C000050364

Easy Walking

in
South Bedfordshire
and
the North Chilterns

Clive Brown

The Book Castle

To Angela
With thanks for the help, encouragement and inspiration.

First published June 2008
by The Book Castle
12 Church Street
Dunstable
Beds LU5 4RU

ISBN 978-1-903747-91-9

Also by Clive Brown

The 'Walking Close to' series of guides including

Walking Close to Woburn Abbey
Walking Close to the Great Ouse near Bedford
Walking Close to the Great Ouse north of Milton Keynes
Walking Close to the Thames near Oxford
Walking Close to Woodstock and Blenheim Palace
Walking Close to the Vale of White Horse
Walking Close to Grafham Water
Walking Close to the Cam and the Granta near Cambridge
Walking Close to the Nene near Northampton
Walking Close to the Lee Valley near Hertford
Walking Close to Epping Forest

Designed and typeset by Tracey Moren, Moren Associates Limited. www.morenassociates.co.uk

Printed in Great Britain by T J International Limited, Padstow, Cornwall

Cover photograph looking past Pitstone Windmill towards Ivinghoe Beacon © Clive Brown

Contents

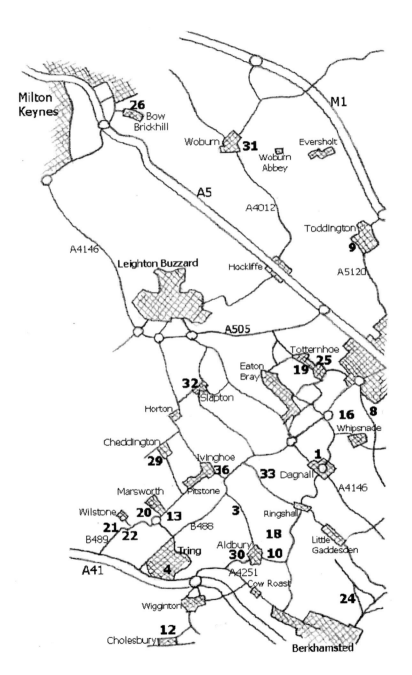

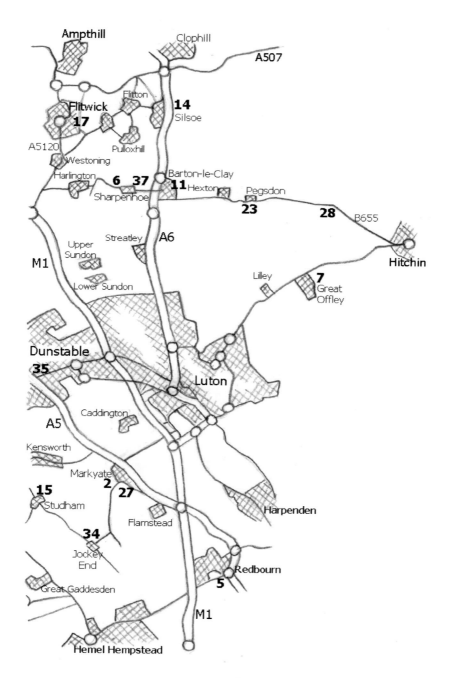

Introduction

The Northern Chilterns and the southern part of Bedfordshire are a well kept secret. While other areas and regions of this country have a deserved reputation for being excellent walking country, this part of the world has hidden away, guarding its beauty and its diversity. Thick wooded slopes, rolling chalk downland, steep hillsides with terrific views at the top. Tranquil towpaths alongside canals with the occasional narrowboat chugging past. Peaceful undulating farmland and sleepy picturesque villages. It sounds idyllic and I believe local people have been keeping quiet about this glorious part of our countryside so that they can keep it to themselves. The major drawback with this book is that more of the public will come and enjoy it.

You will notice of course that the M1 motorway goes through the centre of the area; the busy A5 runs parallel to it and the junction where the A505 joins the A5 in Dunstable can be a real problem. Luton Airport is on the south east corner and jet noise will be in the background of some of the walks. From the top of Ivinghoe Beacon you can hear the Pendolinos sprinting along the West Coast Main Line Railway.

This is modern life and the advantages of this part of the world outweigh these minor inconvenient intrusions.

The book presents a comprehensive guide to the best walks in this locality; the routes use paths, bridleways, rights of way, National Trails and canal towpaths. Some background information and nature notes are included after the walk directions. All the walks are circular; some are in areas already popular with walkers, others are in areas less popular and perhaps less accessible.

South Bedfordshire and the North Chilterns

The area covered in this book is dominated by the chalk ridge escarpment of the Chiltern Hills. Not particularly high in comparison to other ranges of hills in this country, they nevertheless tower over the flatter land to the north and the lower south eastern end of the Greensand Ridge around Woburn. The Chilterns stretch from close to Hitchin, for fifty miles south west, down to the River Thames at Goring. This classic formation of an escarpment has its steep side to the north west and the shallower slope down to the south east. The highest point of 876ft/267m is at Haddington Hill near Wendover. The greater part of the Chilterns has been an Area of Outstanding Natural Beauty (AONB) since 1965.

The Greensand Ridge is one of a series of sandstone ridges across south east England; it runs from north east of Leighton Buzzard into Cambridgeshire. The sandstone here has a greenish tinge caused by a mineral called glauconite; this often decays into a yellowy stain. The ridge is highest around Woburn and is generally covered with conifer trees and sandy heaths.

The northernmost parts of the Chilterns tend to be downland with very little tree cover; further south particularly the Ashridge Estate and other parts outside the scope of this book are swathed in deciduous forests.

The local geography has of course affected transport systems throughout the hills, in the first instance helpfully as the ancient tracks across the hills used higher routes, away from the valley bottoms where softer ground often made the land impassable in bad weather. The Romans built their major road to the north west through the town of Durocobrivis (Dunstable) on the course of another ancient trackway. The Victorian Midland Railway Line and the modern M1 Motorway both keep close to this point. Further west the canal engineer William Jessop chose to take the Grand Junction Canal through the Tring Gap by a series of Locks. Robert Stephenson also used the Gap for the London and Birmingham Railway by the excavation of a deep cutting to keep the gradients down to a level manageable by less powerful early steam engines. The A41 dual carriageway (once the Roman Akeman Street) now traverses the Gap slightly higher up the slope than the original road (since renumbered as the A4251).

Not as intrusive as it once was, the eastern end of the Chilterns has the constant background of the movement of airliners in and out of Luton, the country's seventh largest Airport. The facility opened in

1938 and was even then thought of as a northern terminal for London. It was used by the RAF during the Second World War and has had a chequered history since then; the Airport now handles six and a half million passengers every year. Smaller private aircraft may be seen above the Chilterns but close to Dunstable you are much more likely to see a glider soaring effortlessly above the Downs from one of England's oldest and most popular gliding clubs.

The splendour of Woburn Abbey is repeated in the majestic settings of Ashridge House and Mentmore Towers. Other impressive stately homes were built at Wrest Park, Markyate Cell and Gaddesden Place. Baron Mayer de Rothschild built Mentmore in the early 1850s. It was the first of several properties in the Buckingham/Hertfordshire area owned by the Rothschild family. The houses at Tring, Aston Clinton, Halton, Waddesdon and Ascott (including Mentmore) have all passed into other hands.

Numerous locations in the north of the hills bear the scars of extensive quarrying. Sundon and Totternhoe have large sites that have been closed or worked out; those that have not been commercially reclaimed are now reverting back to nature. Quarrying continues at a site north of Totternhoe and the vast site between Dunstable and Kensworth. The products of these quarries included building stone, lime for agriculture or building and whiting for various uses including decorating materials and the marking of sports fields. Cement has been the most common product of these excavations and is still in local production.

Prehistoric man has also left his mark on some of the highest parts of the range. Traces of ancient agriculture have been found in what are called strip lynchets or cultivated terraces on fairly steep slopes. Evidence of ramparts of Iron Age fortification exists at Ivinghoe Beacon, Sharpenhoe Clappers, Maiden Bower near Totternhoe and Cholesbury.

The Countryside Code
Please take care of the countryside
your leisure is someone's livelihood

Close gates
Start no fires
Keep away from livestock and animals
Do not stray from marked paths
Take litter home
Do not damage walls, hedgerows or fences
Cross only at stiles or gates
Protect plants, trees and wildlife
Keep dogs on leads
Respect crops, machinery and rural property
Do not contaminate water

All of the walks contained in the book can easily be negotiated by an averagely fit person. Some of the routes cross fields which may have a crop growing in them. If the field has been cultivated it is the farmer's responsibility to reinstate the path as quickly as possible. The track may be muddier than normal; the text should give warning of this. I recommend that good quality walking boots are worn; it will make the going easier although they are not absolutely essential. Carry something to drink particularly in hot weather and it's a good idea to have a small snack to eat on the way. Stiles and some paths can get overgrown during the summer months, so folding secateurs are a handy thing to carry in a rucksack.

Very few of the walks use roads, but at some points there is no alternative. Please be careful and use grass verges where possible. If using the road itself, walk on the right hand side facing the oncoming traffic but beware of blind right hand corners.

The information boxes give suggestions on where to park, but sometimes a vehicle will just have to be left on the side of the road. Please park courteously with regard to local residents and passing traffic. It would be good to say that all the walks are easily accessible by bus; sadly this is not the case. The reality is that the further you get into the countryside the more problematic access to buses becomes. Some town centre walks are easy, walks starting in Dunstable, Redbourn, Tring,

Markyate and Flitwick have regular bus connections. Other starting points may be on a bus route, please check local timetables for up to date information.

There are numerous other possibilities for walking within the area covered by this book. The Ashridge Estate has countless paths radiating in all directions; the towpath of the Grand Union Canal is accessible right through the area. The long distance Hertfordshire Way, Greensand Ridge and Icknield Way footpaths, as well as the Ridgeway National Trail all pass through the area on good, well marked paths and tracks.

The maps all have north at the top, unless specified, and give an accurate portrayal of the area though some features may have been emphasised to reflect their importance to the view from ground level. They are close to 1:25 000 in scale but not constant as scale has been sacrificed in some cases for the sake of clarity and to fit restrictions of page size. Distances and times quoted are approximate, time particularly is often subject to weather conditions and whoever is doing the walking. The routes have all been recently walked and surveyed; temporary changes can occur so please follow any signed diversions. The author would appreciate details of any problems encountered, (care of The Book Castle).

I feel that it would be difficult to get lost with the instructions and maps in this book but I do recommend the carrying of an Ordnance Survey Map. Roads, geographical features and buildings not on our map but visible from the route can easily be identified. The larger scale Explorer maps are best; the walks appear on map numbers 181, 182, 192 and 193. Landranger Maps cover at a smaller scale; map numbers 165 and 166.

Thanks to John, Nigel, Sue and Gerry for companionship on several of the walks and their help and encouragement.

Ordnance Survey licence
Reproduced from Ordnance Survey Mapping on behalf of The Controller of Her Majesty's Stationery Office. (C) Crown Copyright Licence No 100037980.

1 Hoo Wood

Dagnall – Studham – Hudnall – Little Gaddesden

6¾ Miles	3¼ Hours

Location and parking Dagnall village is SSW of Dunstable at the junction where the A4146 between Leighton Buzzard and Hemel Hempstead crosses the B4506 between Dunstable and Berkhamsted. No car park, use a sensibly located roadside space.

Grid Reference SP992164

Ordnance Survey Explorer Map no 181, the eastern half of the walk also appears on Explorer no 182. Landranger Map nos 165 and 166.

Facilities No toilets. Small shop and two local pubs, the 'Golden Rule' and the 'Red Lion'.

Start The roundabout at the crossroads.

Description A fairly easy walk on mostly good paths over undulating country, two noticeable slopes to go up. Some stiles and open fields which may be under cultivation. The route passes close by Whipsnade Zoo between points **3** and **4**.

The Walk

1 From the roundabout, take Main Road South (the A4146) towards Hemel Hempstead; follow the roadside path to the multi-directional sign on the far side of the school. Turn left up the path between the fence and the hedge up to the road and turn right for 140yds to the signpost on the left.

2 Turn left through the gate; follow the fence left through the kissing gate and up the slope between fences. Continue past the brick gateposts, through the wide kissing gate and ahead over the golf course. Bear slight left at a marker post, past the marker post at a clump of trees and on to the next marker post.

3 Turn left across the course taking care crossing any of the fairways, keep direction through tree lines and past tall marker posts. Go through the hedge at the last marker post and turn right between the hedge and the chain link fencing enclosing the zoo. Turn left at the fence corner still between the fence and the hedge up to the top corner, turn right and carry on through the trees to the T-junction of paths.

4 Take the track right, along the field edge with the hedge to the left, through the dip and into the trees at the far corner. Bear left along the path through the trees to the corner of the fence on the right.

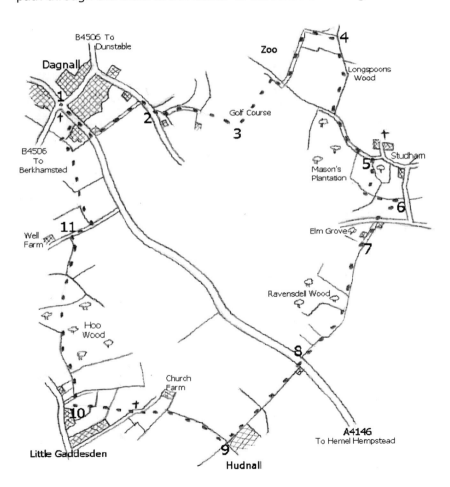

5 Turn right, step over the stile part way along the fence and walk up the field edge to the marker disc. Bear slight right and cross over the stile ahead next to the wide metal gate. Turn left up the field edge through the metal gate and keep direction on the left hand field edge nearly to the road.

6 Within this same field turn sharply back and take a diagonal across the field to the opposite corner. This field may be under cultivation but a track should be visible through any crop. Go through the wide hedge gap, over the road and keep ahead past the signpost up the gravelly drive.

7 Continue direction along the fenced track and the left hand field edge with the hedge to the left through the gate at the far end. Carry on between trees with the fence to the right, downhill and bear left through a gap. Maintain direction to the road with the hedge now to the right.

8 Cross and carry on upslope on the left hand field edge, through the first boundary and the wide gap at the top.

9 Take the track along the field edge to the right, with the hedge to the right; step over the stile and bear left over the field to the stile left of the church. Keep ahead between the car park and the churchyard and maintain direction to the stile.

10 Turn right, with the fence to the left, go through the two narrow gates and take the signposted direction between fences to Dagnall Road. Go through the gate and continue ahead on the path along the edge of Hoo Wood. Exit through the metal gate and carry on across the open field and the field edge with the hedge to the left, bear left to the signpost.

11 Take the wide farm track right, between hedges to the next signpost. Turn left up the field edge with the hedge left and cross the section of open field (a track should be well marked) to the marker post right of the hedge end. Bear right across the field to the far corner and turn left past the signs saying footpath with the hedge to the right. Turn right at the end, down to the road and take the roadside path left back to the starting point at the roundabout.

Background Information

Hoo in a place name usually indicates a prominent spur or land on high ground, although Hoo Wood may have originated with the De Hoo family, owners of Luton Hoo during medieval times. There is another Hoo Wood locally; close to Great Gaddesden (walk no 34).

Dagnall has its origins in Anglo Saxon times, the name thought to be derived from the 'land of a man named Daegga'. During the early Middle Ages it is referred to as Dagenhale. The village owes much of its development to its connections with the Bridgewaters and the Brownlows of Ashridge Park, many of its inhabitants living in cottages rented from the estate and working for the Earls or one of their tenant farmers. During the 19th century Dagnall boasted a wide range of shops and trade premises, including a brewery, shoe makers and wheelwrights.

The Zoological Society of London was founded in 1826 by Sir Stamford Raffles; the zoo in Regent's Park opened in 1828 to members of the society, the public were first admitted in 1847. Sir Peter Chalmers, the society's secretary from 1903-35 visited the Bronx Zoological Park in New York and conceived the idea of a similar centre in the countryside close to London. Hall Farm, near Whipsnade, was bought in 1926 and the first animals arrived in 1928. Whipsnade Park Zoo opened on 23rd May 1931, the next day nearly 40,000 people crowded into the new attraction. Now known as ZSL Whipsnade Zoo, the 600 acre park is home to over 6000 animals and is a centre of research and conservation. Several species in danger of extinction have had zoo bred animals released into the wild. Other species have benefited from the zoo's breeding programme; Cheetahs born at the zoo in 1967 were the first bred in captivity. Cheetahs are notoriously difficult for zoos to breed as they have a low genetic variability; all Cheetahs are thought to descend from a group of only 500 animals surviving the last Ice Age.

The Great Whipsnade Railway provides the additional excitement of riding a steam train through the wild animal paddocks. The whistle of the steam engine can usually be heard in busy periods. The railway opened in 1970; it was built using a lot of the infrastructure and equipment of an industrial railway at Bowaters paper mill near Sittingbourne in Kent, which had closed the previous year.

2 Half Moon Lane

Markyate – Flamstead – Pepperstock

6 Miles **3 Hours**

Location and Parking Markyate is on the A5 trunk road, south east of Dunstable at the junction of the B4540 from Luton. There is a small car park on Hicks Road, between the village centre and the A5.

Grid Reference TL062164

Ordnance Survey Explorer Map no 182. Landranger Map nos 165/166.

Facilities No toilets. Shops, pubs and other facilities all close by in the village.

Start The crossroads in the centre of the village

Description An easy, fairly level walk with few slopes. The route crosses the busy A5 at point **4**. The part between points **6** and **7** can be muddy in wet weather; it is also of course quite noisy.

The Walk

1   Leave along Pickford Road; walk up to the signpost for Flamstead and turn left up the slope between the houses. Bear left at the fork in front of the wooden barrier, past the metal gate and along the field edge with the hedge to the left. At the boundary turn left and immediate right to continue direction with the hedge now right.

2   In the corner follow the field edge left and turn right through the hedge gap at the marker post at the next corner. Maintain direction with the hedge again to the left, over the stile in the boundary. Keep ahead at the signpost along the narrow overgrown path between the fence and the hedge. Follow the track right in the corner, step over the stile and continue slight left with the hedge to the left, over the stile right of the corner and on to the road.

3   Turn left down the road, bearing left to the T-junction in Flamstead. Turn right up to the junction at the 'Three Blackbirds' and take the High Street to the left. At the 'Spotted Dog' turn left down River Hill and follow this road down to the A5.

4 Cross this busy road carefully and continue straight on up Chad Lane, turn right along the old A5 and immediate left again uphill, still on Chad Lane.

5 At Chad Lane Farm turn right over a stile and walk diagonally away from the road through a gate and along the field edge with the hedge to the right. Step over the stile in the corner and keep ahead through the dip, carry on uphill over a stile and across a narrow strip of land which may be under cultivation although a path should be well marked. Keep direction with the trees again to the right along the farm road and over the stile left of the gate; go down the steps to the road.

6 Turn left for 350yds to the signpost on the right and walk across the field nearly to the motorway (a track should be visible within any crop) a farm trailer with an advertisement on was there at the time of survey.

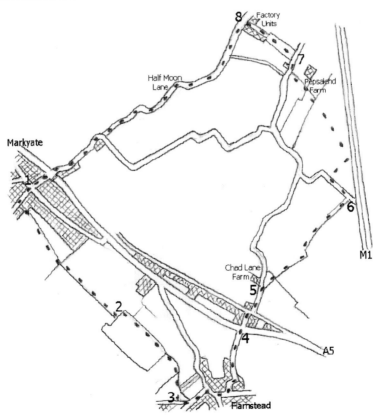

Turn left, still in the same field and cross the stile in the fence ahead, keep direction along this field edge with the fence, then the hedge to the right all the way to the road. Turn right along this road which is a continuation of Chad Lane but now called Pepsal End Road.

7 Carry on to the footpath signpost on the left and cross the stile, take the wide fenced track through the field and keep ahead over the stiles, past the firework factory and out through the wide green gates.

8 Turn left along Half Moon Lane, the wide hardcore byway between hedges. Follow this track all the way to the tarmac road at a corner and keep direction over the footbridge across the busy A5 into Markyate and your starting point.

Background Information

The A5 is one of England's oldest roads; a prehistoric trackway ran between the places that became St Albans and Canterbury. The Romans, very soon after the invasion, wanting good roads for the easy movement of their troops, made this track into a 'via strata' or street. The Romans used the word to describe any paved road, rather than our present use of the word as a road in a built up, populated area. The word strata derives from the layers of material used in the construction.

The Roman road ran from Dubris (Dover) to Viroconium (the modern town of Wroxeter, more important than Shrewsbury in Roman times).

In AD61 a major battle took place at an unknown point somewhere close to the road. The Roman General, Gaius Suetonius Paulinus defeated the forces of Bouddicca, Queen of the Iceni, destroying any further British resistance.

Along with other signs of Rome the road deteriorated during the dark ages and it became known as Waeclinga Street or the 'Street of the Foreigners', (the Romans).

When the Danelaw was created by King Alfred after his defeat of the Danes, Watling Street became the border between the two territories.

In 1706 Watling Street was changed to turnpike status, enabling tolls to be charged against the upkeep of the road, (this continued until 1875).

After the Act of Union in 1801 the London to Shrewsbury section was upgraded and the road extended, with some major engineering work by Thomas Telford, through North Wales to the port of Holyhead to ease travel between London and Dublin.

Several of the towns on the road including Markyate, Redbourn and Dunstable, had a considerable infrastructure dependent on assisting travellers. Inns, hotels and stables, then garages.

The development of motorways in Mainland Europe followed quickly on from the invention of the motor car. The first motorway had been built in Italy in 1921 and the first German autobahn opened 10 years later in 1931 (predating the Nazi regime with which they have always been associated). The building programme proceeded very slowly until the advent of Hitler as German leader. He saw them as a huge status symbol as well as an enormous asset in moving troops quickly around the country, hence the widespread, but wrong opinion that they were a Nazi idea.

Motorways came to Britain a lot later, during 1958, with the construction and opening of the Preston Bypass, later part of the M6, (the Ministry of Transport couldn't decide how to number Motorways for another year). A ceremony was held at Slip End, near Markyate, on the 24th March 1958 to mark the beginning of construction work on the London to South Yorkshire Motorway. The M1 was completed in 1959 and opened on November 2nd. It had been built in two sections, the southern half by Tarmac Construction and the northern part by John Laing; two still well known and respected names in the construction industry.

The system of numbering roads in this country began in 1923. The government realised with the increase in road traffic after World War I, that they were going to have to spend a lot more money on roads. A scheme was introduced to classify roads with A and B followed by a number, the lower the number the more important the road.

The Great North Road between London and Edinburgh was given the classification A1, the other five most important roads in England and Wales were numbered clockwise from London, although the A6 actually started from the A1 in Barnet.

The roads within these segments were numbered with regard to their importance. Originally all roads in a segment were planned to start with the same number, between the A4 and the A5 would start with 4, the roads between the A5 and the A6 would start with 5. In practice several roads ignore this rule and there has been quite a lot of renumbering with changes to traffic patterns since the advent of motorways; parts of the A5 have now become the A5183.

3 Bridgewater Monument

The Ridgeway National Trail – Aldbury – Bridgewater Monument – Ashridge Estate – Ivinghoe Beacon

---

7½ Miles   3¾ Hours

Location and Parking Use the car park on the minor road south east of Ivinghoe village on the way to Aldbury.
Grid Reference SP955149
Ordnance Survey Explorer Map no 181; Landranger Map no 165.
Facilities None. Parking only.
Start From the car park.
Description The walk uses part of the Ridgeway National Trail, goes through picturesque Aldbury and the Ashridge Estate passing close by the Bridgewater Monument which can be seen from various points during the walk. An optional detour goes to the summit of Ivinghoe Beacon. There are several moderately steep slopes.

The Walk

1 Walk out of the car park through the gate at the back and take the path straight on over the hill, continue down the slope and keep ahead upslope again on the obvious Ridgeway Path.
2 At the marker post at the top, above the quarry site, bear left downhill along the line of Grim's Ditch down to the line of trees at the kissing gate.
3 Go through and take the path through the trees for two thirds of a mile, descend the steps to the signpost marked Ridgeway to the right. Turn right and follow the path left to the junction. Bear left still on the Ridgeway, through the trees to a crossroads of paths.
4 Turn left on the path between fences then hedges to the kissing gate. Take the path right, signposted Aldbury and continue down the path left of the farm to the road. Turn left past the church into Aldbury

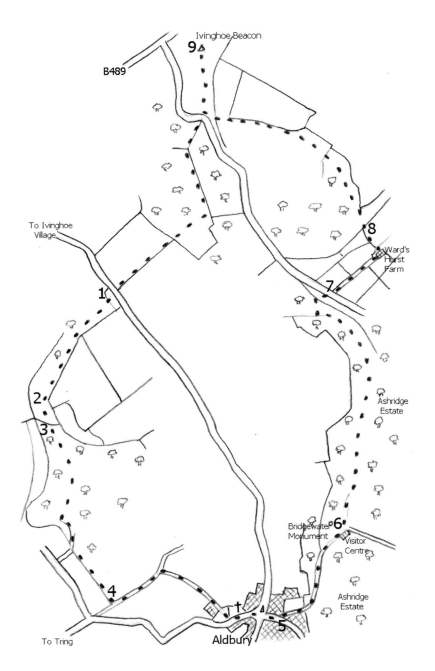

Ivinghoe Beacon

B489

9

To Ivinghoe
Village

1

2

3

4

8

Ward's
Hurst
Farm

7

Ashridge
Estate

Bridgewater
Monument

6

Visitor
Centre

Ashridge
Estate

5

To Tring

Aldbury

village and keep ahead along Tom's Hill Road.

5 Bear left at the signpost for the Bridgewater Monument and keep ahead uphill on the stepped path. Bear left and then right on the major track past the visitor centre to the monument.

6 Keep the original direction on the hardcore path away from the monument and follow this path, which is bearing slowly left, for a mile to a crossroads marked by yellow arrows. Turn right upslope, bearing right to the road at a signpost.

7 Carry on ahead over the road, across the cattle grid and up the double concrete track farm road and into the farmyard at Ward's Hurst Farm. Bear left past a marker post and right with the duckpond to the left. Go through the narrow gate and bear left with the fence and the pond to the left and go through the kissing gate.

8 Take the path downhill through the trees and carry on along the obvious path past posts marked Icknield Way, all the way to the kissing gate at the edge of the trees. Continue ahead on the track past the marker post, keeping the fence to the right up the slope to the stile. Step over and turn right along the path to the top of Ivinghoe Beacon.

9 Retrace steps down to the signpost at the road, cross and bear left up the slope through the bushes and the trees. Step over the stile next to the wide wooden gate and carry on downslope to the marker post. Bear right and keep direction on the obvious track back to the car park ahead.

Background Information

The Monument is inscribed:-

IN HONOUR OF

FRANCIS THIRD DUKE OF BRIDGEWATER

FATHER OF INLAND NAVIGATION

1832

It is 108ft high and has 170 steps inside leading to a viewing gallery; the monument can be visited weekends and bank holidays April - October.

The Egerton family had been Earls of Bridgewater since 1615; the fourth Earl, Scroop Egerton was created Duke in 1720. Francis was born in 1736 the seventh child and fourth son of his second marriage. On the first Duke's death in 1744 his eldest son, John, became the 2nd Duke. John died only 4 years later and Francis at the age of twelve inherited as the 3rd Duke. He was a frail and unloved child and spent a lot of time at Tatton Park in Cheshire, the house of a relative. Visits to his local estate at Worsley where coal mining was in its infancy, would have given him an insight into the problems faced transporting coal to the manufacturing town of Manchester. On leaving Eton he was sent on a 'Grand Tour' of Europe, something of a fashion for young men in those days. The tour, mainly to Italy, was supposed to give him firsthand experience of the arts and classics on the continent. The biggest impression however was made by the Royal Languedoc Canal (now the Canal du Midi) a colossal 17th century engineering feat built to link the Atlantic at Bordeaux with the Mediterranean cutting out the long journey around Spain. The Duke returned to London and fell head over heels for the widowed Duchess of Hamilton. They became engaged, but in a dispute over her sister, the Duke ended the relationship and retired to his estate in Worsley and for the rest of his life shunned society in general and women in particular.

It is interesting to reflect what impact Elizabeth Gunning has made on history; if the Duke had married her would he have pushed the building of canals quite so relentlessly? She was born in 1733 in Huntingdonshire into a poor family; she and her elder sister Maria, both acknowledged as remarkably beautiful women, became actresses. By contemporary accounts they spent some time in the early 1750s looking for rich husbands. At a society function in 1752 Elizabeth met the 6th Duke of Hamilton and they were married the same night. A daughter and two sons were born to the couple but the Duke died in 1758. During the year the Duchess was briefly engaged to the Duke of Bridgewater, but the relationship foundered, (it is thought that the Duke disliked Maria and wanted the Duchess to have no more to do with her). In 1759 the Duchess married the Marquess of Lorne and became Duchess of Argyll when her husband succeeded to his father's title in 1770. Two of the sons of her first marriage became Dukes of Hamilton and two of the sons of her second marriage became Dukes of Argyll. From her poor beginnings Elizabeth had married two Dukes and became the mother of four more. Her sister also married well, to the 6th Earl of Coventry, but died in 1760 of blood poisoning, the victim of using too much lead based makeup.

4 Grim's Ditch

Tring – Hastoe – Grim's Ditch – Wigginton – Tring Park

6¼ Miles   3 Hours

Location and Parking Use the Market Place car park in Tring, (pay and display).
Grid Reference SP925115
Ordnance Survey Explorer Map no 182; Landranger Map no 165.
Facilities Toilets at the car park entrance; all other facilities close by in the town.
Start The car park entrance.
Description One tough slope on the way out and the corresponding slope down on the way back. The route passes through woods and farmland, returning through Tring Park.

The Walk

1 Leave by the vehicle entrance and turn right along the High Street, turn left into Langdon Street and right along King Street. Continue into Park Road up to the footpath signpost on the left. Bear left up the footpath between the fence and the trees, through the wooden gate and the metal kissing gate at the end. Bear right to the bottom left corner on to the road.

2 Turn left, beneath the A41, keep straight on at the fork bearing right with the road and take the byway to the left, past the 'Unsuitable for Motors' sign. Continue past the concrete post bollards on the narrower track between hedges to the T-junction and turn right, over the hump and down to the next T-junction.

3 Take the byway left upslope; keep on this path uphill past the marker post and bear left still uphill at the second marker post. Carry on through the metal barriers to the road at a corner.

4 Turn left along the road into Hastoe village and take the byway, Browns Lane to the right, for a third of a mile to the signpost on the

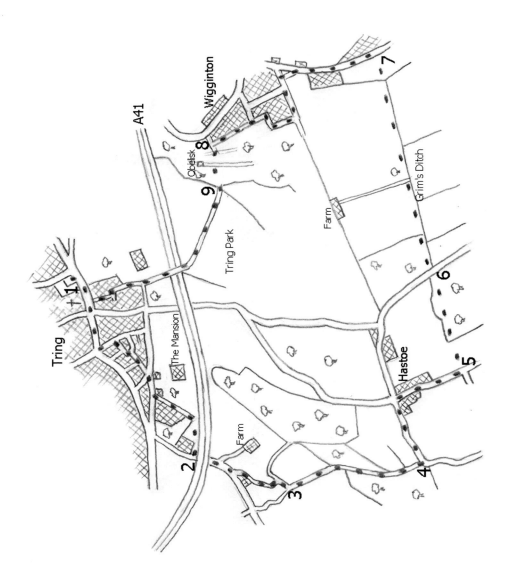

Tring

Wigginton

A41

Obelisk

Tring Park

The Mansion

Farm

Grim's Ditch

Hastoe

Farm

1
2
3
4
5
6
7
8
9

right.

5   Cross the open field to the left, this field may be under cultivation but a path should be well marked. Go through the gap and into the trees and with Grim's Ditch to the left, follow the path ahead to the road.

6   Cross and keep direction along the edge of the trees, left of the Ditch; go through the kissing gate on the right at the end of the path. Continue ahead over the field and exit through the kissing gate to the road.

7   Turn left and walk into Wigginton village; bear left at the footpath signpost along the edge of the sports field to the road and turn left. Keep straight on, up a slight rise, on to the hardcore farm road and turn right at the signpost for Tring Park. Carry on between fences along the back of the bungalows; follow the path right and left, across the access road to the Ridgeway signpost.

8   Go up the track for the short distance to the signpost where the Ridgeway turns left; bear left past the yellow arrow on the marker post downslope on a feint path through the trees. Cross the track (the obelisk is off to the right) and maintain direction further downhill.

9   At the bottom, bear left, go through the kissing gate and bear right, across Tring Park to the footbridge.   Cross back over the A41 and continue up the path to the road, keep direction along the path slight right between the chain link fencing and the flint wall. Turn left and right, down to the High Street to find the car park and the starting point.

Background Information

Grim's Ditch is an earthwork visible in places for a stretch of nearly twenty five miles through parts of Hertfordshire and Buckinghamshire. Archaeological work in the 1970s suggested that it was built during the Iron Age. The name is possibly Saxon in origin; Grim was a nickname given to the God Woden in Anglo-Saxon Mythology. Anything the Saxons didn't understand they attributed to the work of Gods. The ditch is not thought to have been built for defensive purposes; it is more likely a marker between the territories of two local tribes for the containment of sheep and cattle. Some experts believe however, that the ditches nearer to Cholesbury may be part of the Iron Age fort within the village.

Tring Park has long associations with the Rothschild banking family. The house was built during the Restoration, to a Christopher Wren design, but very little of the original house remains. The estate was bought in 1872 by Lionel Rothschild who made considerable alterations to accommodate his lavish style of entertainment. Lionel's grandson Walter, in 1889, started a collection of zoological specimens which grew into a national treasure; it was opened to the public in 1892 and was left to the nation as part of the Natural History Museum. It is now known as the Natural History Museum at Tring. Walter also kept exotic animals and used to be pulled around Tring in a small cart by a Zebra; he also used a larger team of Zebras to haul a carriage around central London.

The Park was effectively cut in two with the building of the A41 Tring bypass in 1975. The house, now known as Tring Mansion and occupied by an Art School is on the town side and the park which is owned by Dacorum Council is on the other side linked by a footbridge to the town. The 300 acre parkland is looked after by The Woodland Trust.

The obelisk in the park is known as Nell Gwynne's Monument, it is thought unlikely that she ever visited the estate and the reason behind the name has been forgotten.

The high ground close to the corner at point 4 is at 245m/803ft the highest point in Hertfordshire. The county border runs along the road in front of the corner and the higher ground to the right is in Buckinghamshire, although not the highest point in that county.

Nature Notes

One of the more unusual inhabitants of the park is the Glis-Glis or Edible Dormouse; it was introduced in 1902 by Walter and is now resident within a 25 mile radius of Tring. It is a miniature (6 inches long) version of the Grey Squirrel, complete with bushy tail.

5 Redbourn Common

Redbourn – The Nickey Line – Norrington End

---

6 Miles   3 Hours

Location and Parking   Use the car park on High Street in Redbourn. There is also a car park on the common near the cricket pitch and roadside parking on Dunstable Road, north of High Street, the old A5 near point **5**.

Grid Reference   TL108123

Ordnance Survey   Explorer Map No 182, Landranger Map No 166.

Facilities   Toilets adjacent; all other facilities close by in the town.

Start   From the car park entrance.

Description   An easy walk, starts along the track of the disused Nickey Line railway

---

The Walk

1   Turn left from the car park entrance and walk down to Waterend Lane, turn left and carry on along the hardcore/gravel surface. Cross the bridge at the ford, go round the double bends and up the slope; descend the steps to the Nickey Line footpath. Turn left along this wide hedged track to the roundabout.

2   Cross the road to the right, this side of the roundabout (the A5183) and the road at right angles (Redbourn Lane, the B487) and continue past the information board further up the Nickey Line for just over half a mile to the marker post.

3   Take the track left downslope between fences and join the wider track straight on. Follow this track left to the marker posts and carry on right/ahead past the yellow disc on the marker post. Cross the metal footbridge and bear left along the edge of the golf course. Go past the marker post and turn right at the marker post in front of the kissing gate.

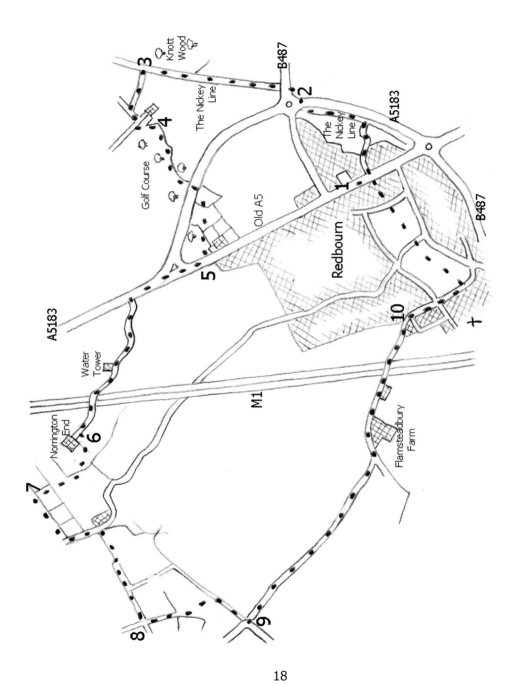

4 Continue along the path through the edge of the trees, then the edge of the golf course for 200yds to a marker post and bear left through the trees to the road (the A 5183). Cross this busy road carefully and go up the steps and over the stile the other side. Bear right across the field and keep direction through a hedge gap then a fence gap to the old A5.

5 Turn right; keep ahead on the narrow path through the trees and the roadside path to Redding Lane. Turn left and follow the road over the M1 to Norrington End.

6 At the signpost, turn left through the kissing gate and cross over to the marker post. Turn right and step over the stile, keep ahead down the slope with the trees to the left and turn left through the kissing gate. Turn right and continue direction downslope with the hedge and trees now right, carry on over the stiles to the signpost at the bottom.

7 Take the track left along the field edge to the road and turn left for 175yds to the signpost on the right, turn right signposted Trowley Bottom on the track at the field edge with the tall hedge to the right. Bear right at the gap then left in the original direction, along the narrow path and carry on to the signpost.

8 Turn left uphill between fences through the gate at the top and continue up the right hand field edge to the marker post. Turn left across the open field, which may be under cultivation although a path should be well marked within any crop. Go through the hedge gap and turn right along the wide tree and hedge lined bridleway to the junction at a road corner.

9 Turn left past the concrete blocks and a metal barrier up the wide farm road between fields, all the way to the marker post at the junction where the hedges start. Fork left past Flamsteadbury Farm and back over the M1 to the edge of Redbourn.

10 Bear right with the road down to the roadside sign for West Common; turn left along the path across the Common, between the lines of trees. Follow the path to the end and keep ahead between walls to the High Street, turn left back to the car park and the starting point.

Background Information

Evidence has been found of both Roman and Saxon settlement at Redbourn; the name is a derivative of the Anglo-Saxon for reedy stream. The village first appears in history with the Domesday Book of 1086, where it is listed as Radburne. A Priory was established in the 12th century; human remains were discovered in the village, the monks of St Albans Abbey decided that this was the burial site of the monk Amphilablus, the man who had converted St Alban to Christianity.

The village itself derived a great deal of trade from its position on Watling Street. During the early part of the 19th century there were at least 25 pubs and inns in the village catering for over 80 coaches stopping per day, plus a substantial amount of private traffic. All this business fell away rapidly after the opening of the London and Birmingham Railway in 1837. A similar situation developed during the first half of the 20th century, when businesses catering for motor traffic on Watling Street were badly affected by the opening of the M1 Motorway in 1959.

Redbourn Common has been used by the Cricket Club since 1823, making it one of the oldest clubs in the country, the common was used regularly for cricket matches through the 18th century and there is a recorded occasion of a cricket match taking place there in 1666.

The line of trees either side of the path dates from the middle of the 18th century, the land was owned by the Earl of Verulam until the 1940s when the Earl presented the common to the Parish Council. Part of it had been in use as a golf course and local farmers had been able to use it to graze cattle until 1951.

The Nickey Line was built by the Midland Railway as a railway connection between Hemel Hempstead and Harpenden via Redbourn. The idea for the railway had been around for several years to facilitate the transport of plaited straw from Hemel Hempstead to Luton to be made into hats. The Midland Railway stepped in with the finance to complete the railway and it opened in 1877. The straw plait trade declined due to cheaper foreign imports. The railway, hampered by the refusal of the London and North Western Railway to allow connection of the Nickey Line to the West Coast Main Line at Boxmoor, never lived up to expectations. The last passengers were carried in 1947 and the line was used for freight only until 1968. The line's main customer had been Hemelite, a company based in the Hemel Hempstead suburb of Cupid Green. Ash, created as a by-product in power stations was transported in for the manufacture of building blocks. The line between Boxmoor and Cupid Green was closed in 1968 and the remainder of the line sold to Hemelite, who operated the line privately with an ex-British Railways diesel locomotive until 1979. The line was taken over by the Dacorum and St Albans councils and converted to a footpath and cycleway, opened in 1985. The origin of the name Nickey is difficult to pin down; it can be spelt with or without the 'e'.

The Nickey Line was the location during the 1930s of a bold

experiment using a vehicle known as a Ro-Railer. It was essentially a single-decker bus fitted with an additional set of flanged wheels. The bus could be started from a bus station or central roadside location in a town or city and driven to the nearest rail station. It would stop on a special wooden ramp and lower the flanged wheels on to the rails, then proceeding via the railway and intermediate stations to its destination and another ramp. The flanged wheels were then retracted and the bus driven to the central point of this town by road, the passengers then alighted without a connecting journey. In practice the system did not impress either management or operating staff and the experiment was soon discontinued.

The locomotive purchased by Hemelite was no D8568, a class 17 diesel, one of 117 built between 1962 and 1965. The design was considered to be a failure in service and more locomotives of the older class 20 were later built instead of 17s. The first of the class was withdrawn in 1968; most had been scrapped by 1972, some after less than 5 years service. After the closure of the Nickey Line no D8568 spent time working in Clitheroe in Lancashire before entering preservation. The locomotive is now in a sense 'home' again in the Chilterns; currently under repair on the Chinnor and Princes Risborough Railway.

6 Moleskin and Markham Hills

Sharpenhoe Clappers – Sundon Hills Country Park

> **5¼ Miles** **2½ Hours**
>
> **Location and Parking** Use the car park at Sharpenhoe Clappers, signposted from Sharpenhoe village.
> **Grid Reference** TL 065295
> **Ordnance Survey** Explorer Map no 193, Landranger Map no 166.
> **Facilities** Parking only. The 'Lynmore' pub on the main road in Sharpenhoe village.
> **Start** From the car park.
> **Description** An easy route on good, easily followed paths, one steep slope down and up, walking through farmland, country park and woods.

The Walk

1 Leave the car park away from the road past the National Trust Sharpenhoe signpost. Turn immediate left over the metal barrier and carry on down to the bottom of the slope. Bear left on the path along the field edge, with the slope rising to the left.

2 At the kissing gate turn left over the road, past the gate and continue on the farm track along the left hand field edge with the slope still left. Turn right at the marker post down a gentler slope with the hedge left bearing right with the field edge to the substantial footbridge and turn left.

3 Keep direction with the hedge still left along the left hand field edge; carry on ahead between trees and follow the track right, up to the road. Turn left to the T-junction and take this busier road right for 25yds to the signpost.

4 Turn left along the left hand field edge, through the hedge gap in the corner and turn right, with the hedge now right. Turn left at the top corner go along the field edge, with the trees to the left, over the rise and turn left at the bottom. Walk up the field edge, bearing left to the second marker post and turn right.

5   Follow the wide path overhung by trees, up the slope and go through the narrow wooden gate at the top. Turn left through the wide hedge gap and take the right hand field edge uphill. At the marker post at the top turn left, follow the hedge to the road and turn right for 50yds along the grass verge. Turn left across this busy road through the kissing gate and turn right up to the Sundon Hills car park.

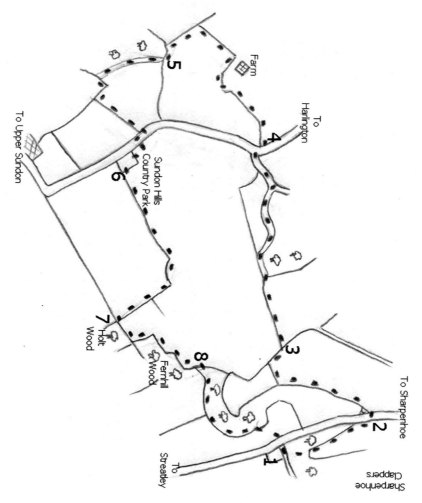

6   Bear left through the kissing gate in the top left corner and keep ahead along the right hand field edge with the hedge to the right. Go down through the wooden kissing gate and turn right, follow the path left and right, around the top of a blind valley. Bear right through the metal kissing gate and keep direction up the field edge trees and hedge to the left.

7   At the top, turn left on the track with Holt Wood to the right; turn left at the far end down to the marker post at the corner and take the track on the field edge to the right, with Fernhill Wood to the right.

8   Turn left in the corner, downslope for 150yds to the hedge gap and turn right. Bear left to a marker post and turn right through the trees on the path at the top of the slope. Keep left at a marker post on a narrower path right at the edge of the slope to a marker post and turn right, through the gap. Turn immediate left through a kissing gate and bear right across the field through the kissing gate in the hedge. Descend the steps and cross to the starting point in the car park.

7 Botanybay Plantation

Great Offley – Hoar's Lane – Botanybay Plantation

4¾ Miles   **2¼ Hours**

Location and parking Great Offley is on the south side of the A505 between Luton and Hitchin. No car park, use a sensibly located roadside space.

Grid reference TL145268

Ordnance Survey Explorer Map no 193, Landranger Map no 166.

Facilities No toilets. Local pubs the 'Gloucester Arms', the 'Green Man' and the 'Red Lion'.

Start The Church.

Description An easy walk along field edges, through woodland and along pleasant bridleways. One noticeable slope down, with the stiff return slope close to the end of the route.

The Walk

1   Facing away from the church, turn left, down to the 'Red Lion' and take the road left past the 'Unsuitable for motors' sign. Follow this hardcore road bearing right, to the signpost and bear slight right along the track on the field edge with the hedge to the right. At the junctions bear slight left between fields to the wide hedge gap.

2   Go through and take a right hand diagonal across the field through the gate in the opposite corner. Turn left along the track on the left hand field edge, through the dip and continue through two more boundaries to the bottom left corner.

3   Turn left through the hedge at the marker post and go through the kissing gate. Keep ahead along the right hand field edge with the fence to the right and through the corner at the kissing gate. Carry on along the field edge with the trees of West Wood to the left, down to the marker post and bear left through the narrow gate.

4   Keep direction along the field edge, bear right on the track through the trees and carry on down the right hand field edge to the road at the corner.

5 Turn immediate left at the signpost along Hoar's Lane and bear right/ahead at the metal gate. Go straight on at the crossroads of tracks at Temple End to the next (unmarked) boundary.

6 Take the field edge left with the hedge to the left (the A505 can be seen longways ahead) and go through the boundary to the marker post at the next corner. Turn left along the wide grass track, under the wires and turn right in the corner for 175yds to the marker post at the next corner. Turn left on the field edge with the hedge to the left up to the corner.

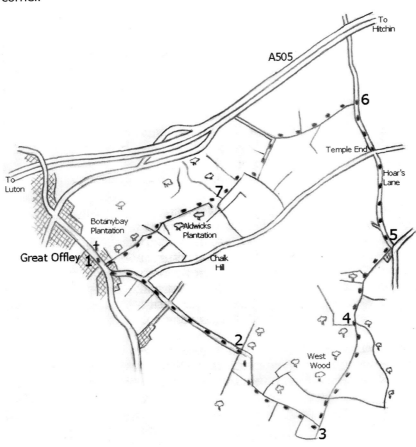

7 Go through and keep direction between the fence and the hedge, pass through this kissing gate and carry on uphill with Aldwicks Plantation to the left. Continue on the path through the trees and along the field edge with narrow Botanybay Plantation to the right. Go past the marker post in the corner and follow the enclosed path to the road, turn right, back to the church and the starting point.

Background Information

Local legends link the Saxon King Offa of Mercia with the area of the village of Offley. Offa came to the Mercian throne in 757, but his succession was disputed by a rival called Beornred. In 758 Offa defeated Beornred in a battle taking place in or near Offley. He then founded a monastery in Hitchin to give thanks for his victory and built a palace in Offley where he is reputed to have died in 796. Very little is known with any certainty about Offa as there were no contemporary chronicles during his reign; the above account was written by Matthew Paris, a monk living in St Albans in the 13th century. He concludes by saying that Offa was buried in a riverside chapel in Bedford which was later washed away in a flood.

It is not even certain that Offa was the builder of the Dyke separating England from Wales. What is beyond question however is that Offa must have been a powerful monarch to have reigned nearly forty years in the 8th century and to have provided the resources needed to build a 150 mile long fortification during the Dark Ages.

He did have a palace and a power base in Tamworth and it is more likely that he died and was buried in that area.

Intriguingly, a gold coin in the British Museum surviving from Offa's time is marked on one side with 'Offa Rex' (King Offa), the inscription on the other side is in Arabic, part of which is upside down!

8 Whipsnade Tree Cathedral

Dunstable Downs – the Tree Cathedral – Whipsnade – Whipsnade Heath – Kensworth

---

4¾ Miles   **2½ Hours**

Location and Parking   The pay and display car park at the Chilterns Gateway Visitor Centre on Dunstable Downs. The walk can also be started from the Whipsnade Heath car park at point **7**, where there are picnic tables but no other facilities.

Grid Reference   TL007197

Ordnance Survey   Explorer Map nos 181 and 182, most, but not all of the walk is on both maps. Landranger Map nos 165 and 166.

Facilities   Visitor Centre has toilets, café and National Trust Gift Shop.

Start   From the Visitor Centre.

Description   An easy walk, some slopes, few stiles, mainly kissing gates. Terrific view from the start. Across the top of the downs, through the solitude of the Tree Cathedral and Whipsnade village, passing close to the scars left by Kensworth Quarry.

The Walk

1   Walk down the slope to the two way signpost at the fence and turn left between the grass and the scrubland. At the corner continue ahead through the longer grass and go through the gate, bear left to the signpost.

2   Keep ahead, slight right with the trees to the left and go through the narrow metal gate.

3   Turn left past the marker post and take the track uphill between hedges for nearly half a mile.

4   At the signpost (easily misread) on the right just past the house on the left, turn left through a narrow fence gap up the path between fences and through the kissing gate. Continue with the fence to the right through the kissing gate midway and the kissing gate at the top

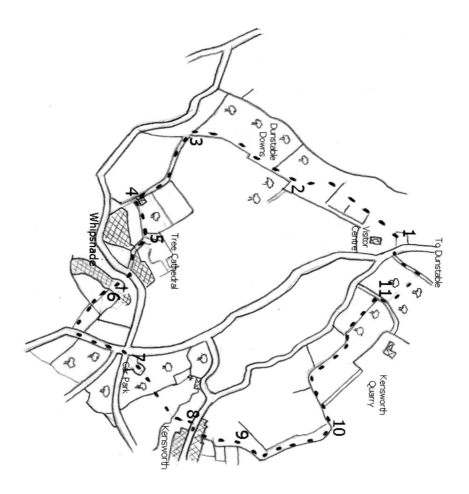

corner.

5 Go into the Tree Cathedral and explore the interior; exit through the car park and walk up to the road. Cross carefully and bear left to the signpost left of the church. Enter the churchyard through the gate, carry on right of the church and go out of the kissing gate at the back.

6 Keep straight on along the field edge with the hedge to the left through the boundary and continue ahead on the right hand field edge with the hedge now right. Pass through the kissing gate at the top, out onto the road, turn left and walk with care along this surprisingly busy road to the roundabout.

7 Bear right and go through the car park, continue through the gate and the picnic area. Keep direction ahead up the path through the trees and the field edge between the barbed wire fence and the tall hedge. Go through the kissing gate and carry on ahead to the road at the edge of Kensworth.

8 Turn right and almost immediate left over the stile at the signpost, go down the enclosed path and turn left through the narrow fence gap. Turn right, back to the original direction, between hedges along the hardcore farm road. Go through the kissing gate on the left and continue ahead downslope with the fence 40yds to the right.

9 Bear right, right of the corrugated iron barn, still downslope with the hedge to the left. Turn left through the kissing gate and follow the left hand field edge as it winds its way up to the next kissing gate by the telegraph pole. Continue along the fold of the bank with the steeper section and the trees to the right, up to the kissing gate at the top corner.

10 Bear left through the trees and turn left with the quarry to the right. Continue between hedges past the marker post and along the left hand field edge bearing right, to the top. Carry on with the hedge and trees still to the left. At the marker post turn left through the gap and immediate right, back to the original direction with the trees now to the right. Walk up to the tarmac access road and turn right for 150yds.

11 Ascend the steps to the left and follow the track downslope through the trees to the marker post. Turn left, then bear left, still on tracks through the trees and go through the barrier. Keep direction to the road and the car park just the other side.

Background Information

The Tree Cathedral is the creation of Edmund Blyth (1898-1969). As a cadet at Sandhurst in 1916, he had been friends with Arthur Bailey and John Bennett. They had both been killed in France in 1918 and Blyth was looking for a suitable memorial to them.

In 1930, Blyth and his wife visited Liverpool cathedral which was still under construction. The building left him with a sense of inspiration and on the way home he saw the sun set through some trees on a Cotswold hillside; the idea of a tree cathedral was born.

Work started on the site in 1932 with the planting of the nave, although the poplars first planted each side of a grassy avenue have since been replaced by lime trees. The work was completed in 1939 but Blyth's second stint in the army during World War II left the cathedral untended and overgrown. With the help of friends the site was renovated and the first service took place in 1953.

The Tree Cathedral was given to the National Trust in 1960; the care and maintenance is looked after by an independent fund.

9 Sundon Quarry

Toddington – Upper Sundon – Chalton

7¼ Miles	3½ Hours

Location and Parking Toddington is on the A5120 half a mile south of Junction 12 on the M1. No car park, use a sensibly located roadside parking space.

Grid Reference TL009288

Ordnance Survey Explorer Map no 193, Landranger Map no 166.

Facilities No toilets. Shops and a good range of pubs, restaurants and takeaways all in the village.

Start From the village green.

Description A fairly level walk with one noticeable slope up and down next to the quarry, some stiles and gates. Several short sections could get very muddy in wet weather.

The Walk

1 Go past the 'Oddfellows Arms', down Conger Lane and turn left through the high kissing gate at the signpost. Bear right over the stile between the moat and the barn, step over the next stile and turn right. Follow this hardcore road downslope, as it bears left go straight on over the field. This field may be under cultivation but a path should be visible within any crop.

2 Cross the road and continue ahead to the yellow top marker post, carry on over the field, a track should be well marked. Cross the footbridge over the River Flit and keep going to the corner of the wood. Turn right along the field edge with the trees to the right; keep direction, changing from right to left hand field edge past the end of Hipsey Spinney. Step over the stile and cross the field ahead (a track should be well marked) to the yellow top post.

3 Go up the slope and cross the bridges over the M1 and the railway. Keep straight on and join the tarmac road uphill, as this road bears right continue ahead between concrete bollards along the road into Upper Sundon. Turn right and follow the road past the landfill entrance to the

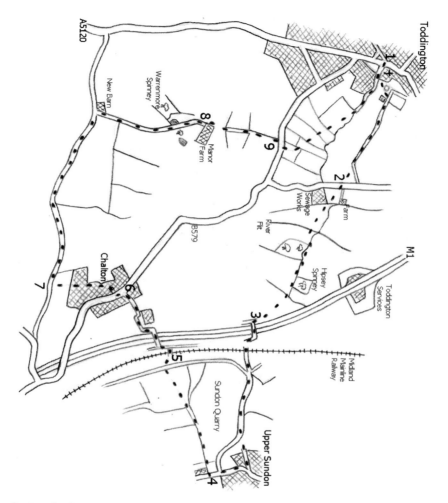

footpath signpost on the right.

4 Pass through the wooden kissing gate and the next two kissing gates on the left hand field edge; follow the field edge with the hedge to the left. Carry on down the slope through the trees, bear left of the pylon and slight left over the field corner to the yellow top post, visible against the trees ahead. Go over the tree lined road and bear right over the field to the footbridge.

5 Cross back over the railway, take the concrete road left and turn right across the bridge over the M1. Follow this concrete then hardcore road left then right; it continues right through a wide gap and left into Chalton village.

6   Cross the road and turn left up to the Chiltern Way signpost, go down the fenced path and bear left of the play area. Continue over the drive and through the kissing gate, carry on along the hedged path and the narrow concrete road. Bear left at the end and turn right, uphill on the estate road, keep ahead past the signpost along the path between houses and follow the track ahead over the field.

7   Turn right along the wide byway between hedges, carry on all the way to the farm and turn right past the footpath signpost. Continue down this tarmac then hardcore farm road all the way to the buildings at Manor Farm.

8   Turn left and immediate right, around the farm; from the corner of the barn keep straight ahead over the field, past the gate and over the footbridge. Carry on up the bridleway between the trees and the fence, cross the stile and continue along the left hand field edge to the road.

9   Turn right for 90yds to the signpost on the left, step over the stile and bear slight left to the next stile. Keep direction over stiles to the bottom right of the long field, continue ahead up the path between trees and narrow Conger Lane into Toddington and your starting point.

Background Information

The wild and derelict Sundon Quarry area, now an important SSSI (Site of Special Scientific Interest), was once a busy place with a large cement works and considerable narrow gauge railway system.

The railway here is the Midland Main Line to London St Pancras, which came onto the scene quite late compared to the neighbouring main lines into London. The West Coast Main Line into Euston opened in 1837 (see notes on walk no 30 Cow Roast). The East Coast Main Line between Kings Cross and the North East was completed in 1852. The route between St Pancras and Bedford did not open until 1868.

The Midland Railway had been formed in 1844, by the amalgamation of three smaller railways in the North Midlands and South Yorkshire. The lines all centred on Derby and that town became the railway's headquarters and site of the locomotive works. All the lucrative traffic from the North East, Yorkshire and the North Midlands was channelled through Midland Railway territory to Rugby where a connection could be made with the London and North Western Railway's line into Euston. This was far from ideal for the Midland. Rugby quickly became a classic bottleneck and the LNWR of course always gave priority to its own passengers and trains.

The advent of the East Coast Main Line in 1852 took away a lot of business from the Midland. The railway turned this situation into an opportunity and constructed a new line from Wigston, just south of Leicester, through the East Midlands and Bedford to join the Great Northern route at Hitchin, so that they could run their own trains directly into Kings Cross. The annual fee for this service was £20,000, then of course a considerable amount of money.

This was another arrangement waiting to go sour. There was friction from the start, with the Great Northern staff naturally favouring their own trains and the Midland realised that their own main line from Bedford through Luton and into London was their only solution.

10 Ashridge Park

Ashridge Park – Little Gaddesden – Hudnall – Berkhamsted Common

---

7 Miles   3½ Hours

Location and Parking   Use the small National Trust parking area in the trees between Aldbury and the B4506.
Grid Reference   SP971119
Ordnance Survey   Explorer Map no 181, Landranger Map no 165
Facilities   Parking only.
Start   From the car park entrance.
Description   A fairly easy walk with some gates and stiles, with an easy slope down and up again. Parts of the walk go through trees, the tracks are normally well used and easy to follow.

The Walk

1   Turn right, out of the car park entrance and walk parallel to the road, past the corner to the signposts for the restricted access to the Ashridge Estate, (walkers are not restricted). Turn left up the estate driveway to the crossroads of paths at the marker post. Take the path right for 80yds, then bear left at a marker post and continue to the B4506.

2   Cross and keep ahead past a marker post; as the trees end on the left, turn left past a marker post and keep ahead past further marker posts. Join the tarmac road right/straight on at the signpost over Prince's Riding to where the road turns left at Old Park Lodge.

3   Keep ahead, right of the barn and through the trees, looking out for any danger from golfers while crossing the fairways. Carry on left of the clubhouse and join the road left/straight on at the signpost.

4   As the road turns left, bear right past a marker post and walk up the wide path between chain link fencing and hedges. Continue through the trees, over another fairway (mind the golf balls again) and downhill through the narrow fenced path. Cross the access road at a signpost

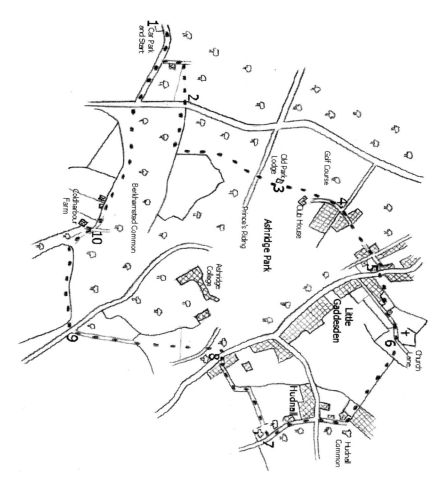

and keep ahead between fences to the road at the 'Bridgewater Arms'.
5 Turn right and almost immediate left through the kissing gate at the signpost, carry on between fences past the bungalows and go through a kissing gate. Bear right through the field and exit over the stile. Turn left along this narrow road (Church Lane) and bear right at the church to the signpost for Hudnall Lane.
6 Step over the stile and cross the field, go through the boundary and bear right along the field edge with the hedge to the left. Go through the metal kissing gate and follow the left hand field edge, through the next kissing gate and along the hedged path. Bear right on the

tarmac driveway with Hudnall Common to the left and cross the road. Keep ahead up the cul-de-sac opposite bearing left to the bridleway signposts.

7 Turn right, on the track through the trees and keep direction between the fence and the trees. Follow the path left then right and carry on, through the farmyard up to the wall. Turn right and immediate left, through a metal gate; go down the walled path to the road in Little Gaddesden.

8 Take the road right for 175yds to the signpost for Ashridge toll road and turn left down the path between low walls to a marker post. Bear left on the faint track through the trees to a marker post at a more substantial track. Keep direction ahead up the grass slope through a narrow gate and pass left of the solitary tree. Continue through the kissing gate along the path between fences down to the road.

9 Cross and bear immediate right between low posts along the bridleway on the field edge with the trees to the right. In the bottom corner, bear right on the track through the trees to the junction and continue to the right, to the crossroads of tracks at Coldharbour Farm.

10 Keep ahead, at Little Coldharbour Farm bear right still on the wide grass track through trees; maintain this direction to the B4506 at the T-junction. Continue ahead parallel to the road, to the parking area on the left.

Background Information

The Bridgewaters came to Ashridge in 1604; Thomas Egerton (1540-1617) was Lord Chancellor for both Elizabeth I and James I; he was made Viscount Brackley in 1616 and died 12 days after he retired. His son John (1579-1649) became the Earl of Bridgewater two months after his father's death.

In 1687 there was a disastrous fire at Bridgewater House in London in which two sons of the third Earl, (John Egerton 1646-1701), died. Scroop Egerton (1681-1744) the third son succeeded to the title. Scroop, (his grandfather was called Emanuel Scrope), became the first Duke of Bridgewater in 1720.

The title was held briefly by his son John (1727-1748) before passing to his younger brother Francis, who succeeded in spite of being the youngest of four brothers; two other brothers had died young. Francis (the Canal Duke) died in 1803, never having married, and the Dukedom became extinct. The Duke left his considerable fortune in a very complicated will to his nephew, other relatives and occupants of the House of Lords.

The Earldom and Ashridge passed to a second cousin John William Egerton who also died without issue, leaving his wife occupying Ashridge until she died in 1848. His younger brother Francis Henry (1756-1829) was a real eccentric. He held dinner parties for his huge assortment of dogs, which were all dressed up in fashionable clothes. He also enjoyed shooting and when his eyes were failing would be supplied with an endless succession of Partridges and Pigeons which had had their wings clipped so they couldn't escape and he couldn't miss.

Ashridge came into the family of the Earls Brownlow, distant relatives of the Bridgewaters (the second Earl changed his name to Egerton-Cust). The Brownlows already owned the Belton Estate in Lincolnshire and when the 3rd Earl died in 1921, again childless, the family retained Belton and sold off the Ashridge Estate. The land went to the National Trust and the house became a college.

11 Barton Hills

Barton-le-Clay – Icknield Way – Barton Hills

4¾ Miles   **2½ Hours**

Location and Parking Barton-le-Clay is bypassed by the A6, 5 miles north of Luton. No car park, find a sensibly located roadside parking space as close to the church as possible.
Grid Reference TL085304
Ordnance Survey Explorer Map no 193, Landranger Map no 166.
Facilities No toilets; shops and pubs in the village (half a mile).
Start The signpost opposite the Church.
Description A few stiles and gates, one long upward slope out and a steep slope down on the return leg through the nature reserve.

The Walk

1 Take the enclosed path away from the signpost opposite the church; go through the kissing gate and cross the playing field on to Old Road and turn left down to the end.
2 Bear left on the narrow path up the slope between hedges, left of the house. Follow this track for a mile, up to the road.
3 Turn left for 100yds to the bridleway signpost and turn right along the left hand edge of the right hand field. Follow this track left and right, over the boundary and up into the wood, Maulden Firs.
4 At the Icknield Way turn left up to the next marker post and take the path left on the field edge uphill, with the hedge to the right. Continue direction to the road; turn right for 160yds to the signpost on the left.
5 Turn left up this fenced path to the Barton Hills information board. Go through the kissing gate and take the path down the steep slope to the valley floor.
6 Continue ahead, bear left down the steps and follow the path, with the stream to the right. Go through a gate and follow a track in the grass through a narrow field into a partial clearing close to the cemetery.
7 Turn right over a metal handrailed footbridge across the stream and out to the field edge. Turn left with the hedge and the cemetery to the

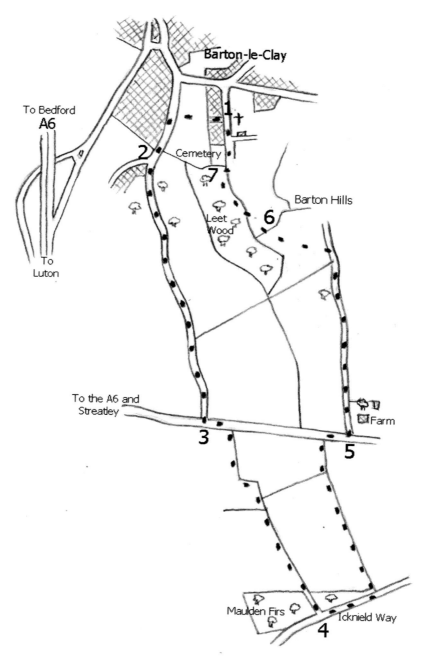

Barton-le-Clay

To Bedford
A6

1

To
Luton

2

Cemetery

7

Barton Hills

Leet
Wood

6

To the A6 and
Streatley

Farm

3

5

Maulden Firs

Icknield Way

4

left, keep direction along the road to the church and the starting point.

Nature Notes

Look out for the Marbled White butterfly which may be seen in the area between June and August. It is unmistakable with its black patterns on a white background. Huge swarms of them can sometimes be seen fluttering over chalk grassland during the summer. It feeds on grasses particularly thistles, Red Fescue and Scabious. Females lay eggs loose in the grass, often while still flying.

The caterpillars, which are lime green with a dark green stripe along the back, hatch in late summer and go into immediate hibernation until late spring when they start to feed on fresh growth.

The species is not threatened, having increased its population in southern Britain over the last twenty five years.

Two other species often seen at Barton Hills are the Chalkhill Blue and the Grizzled Skipper.

The site is also a good place to see the Pasque-flower, (called that because it blooms at Easter time).

12 High Scrubs

Cholesbury – Buckland Common – Grim's Ditch

4¼ Miles   **2 Hours**

Location and Parking Cholesbury village is on minor roads south of Tring and west of Berkhamsted. No car park; there is often space on the common at the eastern end of the village.
Grid Reference SP932071
Ordnance Survey Explorer Map no 181, Landranger Map no 165.
Facilities   No toilets. Three pubs: the 'Full Moon', the 'Rose and Crown' and the 'White Lion' all close.
Start Cholesbury Lane, just east of the junction with Parrott's Lane.
Description   An easy fairly level walk with few stiles and gates.

The Walk

1   Take the footpath signposted between Home Farm Cottage and the Old Rectory. Go through the kissing gate, keep ahead through the kissing gate in the dip and turn right with the barbed wire fence to the right. Continue through the kissing gate in the corner and along the field edge with the hedge to the right. Turn right at the marker post up the slope with the fence, house and garage to the left.
2   Turn left along the hardcore edge of this busy road to the junction and fork right into Bottom Road, turn immediate right up Little Twye Road.
3   After 240yds as the road swings right, step over the stile on the left and bear right over the field which may be under cultivation although a path should be well marked. Cross the hardcore drive and the stile, continue ahead on the right hand field edge, fence and hedge to the right, to the stile. Keep direction, slight left, over the fence and into the trees.
4   Follow the path, there are directional arrows on trees, through the wood; maintain direction and exit through the kissing gate. Keep on

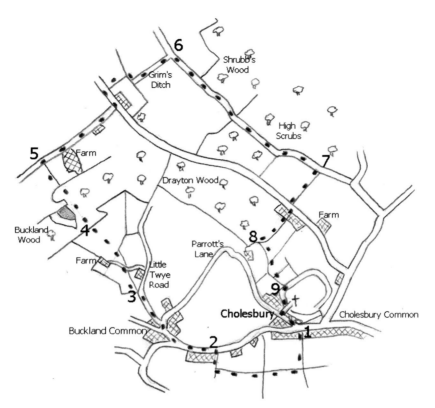

the field edge ahead with the fence to the right and turn right on to the hardcore road.

5   Walk along this road, (the course of Grim's Ditch), through the dip and past the houses to the road. Turn left for 40yds to the signpost on the right and step over the stile, go up the right hand field edge with the hedge to the right and turn right through the gap at the end. Take the path to the left inside the line of trees with Grim's Ditch to the right to the signposts at the more substantial farm road.

6   Turn right along this wide, hedged, hardcore byway and keep direction past Shrubb's Wood and High Scrubs for close to a mile to a crossroads of paths at an easily missed signpost.

7   Turn right over the stile and walk up the field edge with the hedge to the left. Cross the road and keep direction along the footpath slight left, carry on through the trees to the marker post and step over the stile on the left.

8 Go down the right hand field edge through the kissing gate, over the stile; keep ahead through the trees, over another stile and up to the ditch.

9 Turn right, around the fort embankment with the defensive ditch to the left. Go through the kissing gate, on to the Church Drive and turn right, through the gates. Follow the road (Parrott's Lane) left, down into the village and the starting point.

Nature Notes

The Red Kite, a magnificent bird of prey, with a wingspan of five to six feet, can often be seen in the area. It has made a striking comeback from the verge of extinction in the British Isles. This large red/brown bird can be identified by its forked tail twisting to change direction as it soars effortlessly looking for food.

The kite was once commonplace scavenging for food on the streets of medieval and Tudor towns. The population fell drastically, particularly during the 19th century due to the activities of egg collectors and taxidermists. It was also a regular target for gamekeepers who believed all birds of prey hunted game birds.

Until recently the species was limited to a small group of about thirty survivors in central Wales. A programme to reintroduce the species into England started in 1989 when Red Kite chicks which had been reared in Spain were released in the Chilterns on the Wormsley estate of Sir Paul Getty. The programme has been very successful and with further chicks having been released each year there is a large, viable, population in the area. England is now the only European location where Red Kites are increasing rather than decreasing in numbers.

13 Seabrook Locks

Startop's End – Grand Union Canal – Pitstone Windmill – Ivinghoe – Great Seabrook – Marsworth

8 Miles	4 Hours

Location and Parking Use the car park (pay and display) at Marsworth off the B489 between the Grand Union Canal and Startop's End Reservoir.

Grid Reference SP920141

Ordnance Survey Explorer Map no 181, Landranger Map no 165.

Facilities No toilets; café adjacent and pubs the 'Anglers Retreat' and the 'White Lion' on the other side of the B489.

Start From the car park.

Description A fairly level walk with few gates and stiles, using canal towpaths, paths and field edges. There is a short section along the side of the B488 between points **2** and **3**.

The Walk

1 Walk out of the far end of the car park and continue along the canal towpath, past the locks and over the bridge across the Wendover Arm, all the way to bridge no 133 at the 'Grand Junction Arms' pub.

2 Go up to the road and turn left over the canal; follow this reasonably busy road (B488) carefully using the grass verges where possible. Cross over the railway line and carry on up to the signpost on the left just short of the roundabout.

3 Step over the stile; go along the path parallel to the road and cross the road at an angle. Keep direction over the field on the track upslope; there is, towards the end, a hedge on the left. Continue between hedges and bear right up the road, houses to each side.

4 Turn left at the T-junction, along the roadside path to the signpost on the right. Turn right and go through the kissing gate, keep direction

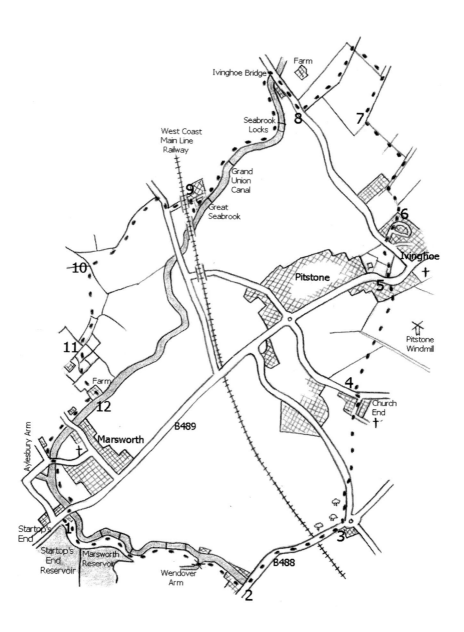

Farm

Ivinghoe Bridge

Seabrook
Locks

8

7

West Coast
Main Line
Railway

Grand
Union
Canal

9

Great
Seabrook

6

Ivinghoe

10

Pitstone

5

✝

✳
Pitstone
Windmill

11

4

Church
End
✝

Farm

12

B489

Marsworth

✝

Aylesbury Arm

1

Startop's
End

Startop's
End
Reservoir

Marsworth
Reservoir

3

Wendover
Arm

B488

2

47

along the path between fields. *The stately house Mentmore can be seen off to the left in the middle distance, Pitstone Windmill, a National Trust property is close by on the right and the prominent hill slightly right ahead is Ivinghoe Beacon.* Go through the gate at the houses ahead up the track and keep ahead to the road.

5   Turn left on the road in Brook End between Ivinghoe and Pitstone, for 30yds to the signpost and turn right through the barriers. Carry on up the path between the fence and the hedge, as the fence ends turn left through the gap. Go over the rough untended field on a diagonal to the road, cross the road on a slight left and continue ahead into Maud Janes Close. At the top corner bear left at the signpost along the enclosed path.

6   Take the left hand field edge ahead to the wide farm track near the barn and turn right. Follow this track as it swings left through the hedge and carry on with the tall hedge to the right. Bear right maintaining direction beneath the electric cables to the corner and cross the stile in the hedge gap.

7   Turn right along the tarmac road to the gateway, go through and turn left; take the path left of the low fence, over the stile in the corner and keep ahead with the hedge and the dyke to the left up to the gateway on the left. Go through and turn left, follow this wide farm track to the right and carry on all the way to the road.

8   Take this surprisingly busy road to the right, go over the bridge and turn left, carry on to the right, along the towpath with the canal to the left. Continue past Seabrook Locks and the next two locks for almost exactly a mile to the swing bridge and step over the stile next to the gate on the right. Bear left then right with the fence to the right and cross the stile near the railway bridge.

9   Go under the bridge, walk up to the T-junction and turn right for 140yds to the signpost. Turn left and go up the right hand field edge with the hedge to the right for 500yds to the marker post. Bear left across the field which may be under cultivation, although a path should be well marked within any crop. Go past the marker post to the stand of trees and cross the stile hidden on the right.

10 Bear left with the trees to the left over the field corner past the wooden railing and bear right, over the metal railed footbridge. Cross the fence marked by a disc, keep ahead up the narrow field and bear left in the corner over the stiles either side of the footbridge.

11 Keep direction across two stiles in fences and the stile in the far corner. Go up the left hand field edge for 50yds and step over the stile to the left. Carry on ahead across this field, over the stile in the hedge gap, through the farmyard and the metal gate to the bridge.

12 Cross the stile on the right, this side of the bridge and join the towpath to the right with the canal again to the left. Continue up to bridge 131, cross and follow the towpath, keeping direction with the canal now right, past the Aylesbury Arm junction to Marsworth and the starting point in the car park by the reservoir.

Background Information

The Bridgewater Canal, Britain's first purpose built canal, was opened in 1761. The construction of the canal solved two major problems for the Duke of Bridgewater who owned a coal mine at Worsley in Lancashire. The canal went into the mine at the same level as the mine workings; the coal was loaded directly into barges to save the time and expense of winding it to the top of the pit. The constant problem of the pit flooding was relieved by the water being directed into the canal. The mine was drained and the canal had a continuous supply of water. James Brindley (1716-1772), the canal's engineer, built the canal on one level with no locks into the centre of Manchester where the price of coal fell by three quarters.

After the success of the Bridgewater Canal, James Brindley envisaged a 'Grand Cross' of canals to link the four great rivers of England – the Mersey, Trent, Severn and Thames. The Oxford Canal, opened in 1790, completed this vision sixteen years after Brindley's death. It was, however, quite a long way round by this route. The Oxford was built as a contour canal; it wound its way around hills on the same level to avoid building locks. The Thames between Oxford and London also left a lot to be desired, poorly maintained compared to a modern canal and suffering from water shortages because mill owners kept the water back for their own use.

The Grand Junction Canal was built between 1793 and 1805; it ran from the Oxford Canal at Braunston in Northamptonshire to the Thames at Brentford, cutting over sixty miles from the Oxford route. It opened to the Tring summit at Bulbourne in 1799; the rest of the canal apart from the tunnel at Blisworth was open from the next year. The tunnel gave the builders a great deal of trouble and a temporary tramway had to be used over the hill until the tunnel finally opened in 1805.

The canal thrived until the opening of the London and Birmingham Railway in 1838, which used much the same route and took away a lot of the canal's business. Canals struggled on through the Victorian era, but the Grand Junction Canal kept busy through its commercial lifetime, charging lower tolls where possible to increase business and traffic flow.

During the late 1920s it became obvious that some kind of rationalisation had to take place and the Grand Junction joined the Regent's Canal and the Warwick Canal in an amalgamation to form the Grand Union Canal.

All canals were nationalised in 1948, the British Waterways Board took over in 1963 and still own and operate most of the inland waterway system in the country. Oddly enough one of the canals not owned by British Waterways is the Bridgewater Canal which was bought by the Manchester Ship Canal in 1885, who still own it.

In the 21st century more narrow boats and other craft use the canals for leisure purposes than were on the canals at the height of the Industrial Revolution.

Aldbury was used as a location for scenes in the 'Bridget Jones' films and several episodes of the cult TV series 'The Avengers'. The village and Ashridge College also appeared in the 1967 film 'The Dirty Dozen'.

14 Wrest Park

Silsoe – Higham Gobion – Wrest Park

5½ Miles   **2¾ Hours**

Location and Parking   Silsoe is bypassed by the A6, a mile south of the junction with the A507, midway between Bedford and Luton. No car park, use a sensibly located roadside space; there is often room near the church on Church Road (towards Wrest Park).
Grid Reference   TL082356
Ordnance Survey   Explorer Map no 193, Landranger Map no 153 & 166.
Facilities   No toilets; shop/post office, newsagents/shop and two pubs the 'George' and the 'Star and Garter'.
Start   From the junction of High Street and Church Road
Description   The route leads through parkland, woods, field edges and estate roads; level walking with few gates or stiles.

The Walk

1   Walk along Church Road past the church, through the blue gateway and over the bridge across the A6. Turn right parallel with the A6 and veer left with the wide track, follow as it twists and turns to the marker post at the entrance to Buckle Grove.

2   Continue over the footbridge and through the trees. At the edge of the wood bear left over the field which may be under cultivation, although a path should be well marked within any crop, to the road. Cross and carry on up the hardcore farm road ahead, pass through the wooden kissing gate and the narrow stand of trees.

3   Follow the right hand field edge with the trees to the right, go through the narrow hedge gap and turn left along the left hand field edge. At the marker post turn right over the field (a track should be visible), cross the footbridge and continue ahead to the marker post. Bear left on the right hand field edge with the hedge to the right. At this next marker post turnright along the farm track with the trees to the left, bear left at the yellow top post through the farmyard and follow the

51

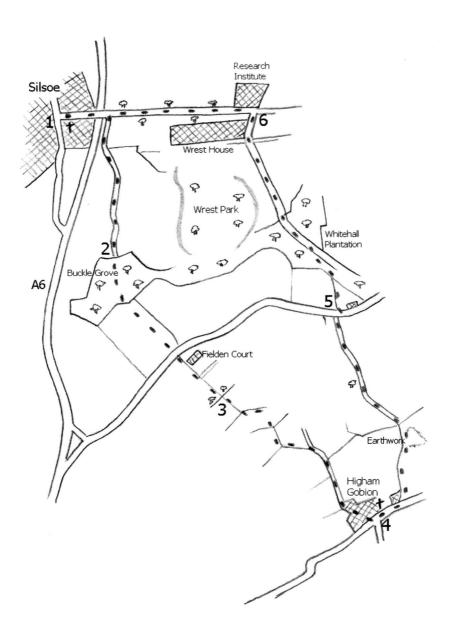

Silsoe

Research
Institute

Wrest House

Wrest Park

A6

Buckle Grove

Whitehall
Plantation

Fielden Court

Earthwork

Higham
Gobion

path through the gate to the road.

4   Turn left for 400yds to the signpost next to the wide metal gate, turn left down the left hand field edge. Go through the gate and follow the track left of the earthworks through the gate at the bottom left. Carry on ahead between fields, passing right of the trees all the way to the road.

5   Cross and continue direction slight right, carry on along the signposted bridleway between the trees and the barbed wire fence. Go over the footbridge and follow the path through the trees of Whitehall Plantation. Bear left at the marker post onto the wider track and keep direction on this estate road between fields. Go through the gateposts and keep right at the buildings.

6   Follow the road left at the signpost and continue past Wrest House through the tree lined avenue into Silsoe to the starting point on Church Road.

Background Information

The present house at Wrest Park was designed by Thomas de Grey (1781-1859), 2nd Earl de Grey from 1833, (not to be confused with the Earl Greys after whom the tea was named, they are a completely different family). He was an amateur architect and the first president of the Institute of British Architects. The house was completed in 1839. The formal gardens close to the house date from the early 18th century and were the work of George London and Henry Wise; the surrounding parkland with its clever use of water features was laid out to a more informal style in 1760 by Capability Brown (1716-1783).

The Grey family has been associated with Wrest Park since the late Middle Ages although their power base seems to have been around the Ruthin area in North Wales. Roger Grey was created 1st Baron Grey de Ruthyn in 1324, his great grandson Edmund (1416-1490), the 4th Baron, was originally a Lancastrian supporter in the Wars of the Roses (1455-1485). At the Battle of Northampton in 1460 Edmund commanded the Lancastrian right flank; as the Yorkist army approached under the command of the Earl of Warwick, Edmund's men simply let them through and the Lancastrian army was routed. Edmund became a fervent Yorkist and was rewarded with the Earldom of Kent in 1465.

The title descended to Henry Grey (1671-1740) who became 12th Earl in 1702, he was elevated to Marquess of Kent in 1706 and Duke of Kent in 1710. The Duke outlived both his sons; his eldest son Anthony had died in 1723, when a grain of barley stuck in his throat. The main titles died with him but his granddaughter, Jemima Yorke was made Marchioness Grey.   This title passed to her grandson Thomas who became the 2nd Earl Grey, the architect who built the new mansion.

Thomas also died childless, passing the Earl de Grey title to his nephew, George Robinson (1827-1909), who was already the Earl of Ripon; his father had been Prime Minister for five months in 1827-8 (George had in fact been born at 10 Downing Street).   Unlike his father who belonged to the Conservative Party, George served in every Liberal Cabinet for nearly fifty years.

In 1917 the Wrest Park estate was sold, ending centuries of occupation by one family.   The last Earl de Grey died at Studley Royal in 1923 and the title became extinct again.

15 Studham Common

Studham Common – Clement's End – Jockey End – Beechwood Park

---

6 Miles   3 Hours

Location and Parking The parking area is east of Studham village on the road between Kensworth and Clement's End. A bar prevents high vehicles from entering.
Grid Reference TL027155
Ordnance Survey Explorer Map no 182, Landranger Map no 166.
Facilities Picnic tables only. No toilets. Two pubs, The 'Red Lion' and the 'Bell' in the village.
Start From the car park.
Description An easy walk through woods, farmland and well surfaced bridleways and tracks. Fairly level, with some stiles and gates.

The Walk

1   Walk out of the back of the car park over the two sleeper footbridge and up the right hand field edge with the hedge to the right. In the corner turn right through the gap and continue along the left hand field edge bearing right. Turn right then bear right through the fence and follow the field edge with the fence to the right, through the fence ahead. Keep direction along the gravel drive to the road.
2   Turn left along the wide grass verge and fork left at the junction into Clement's End Road up to the signpost on the right. Bear right between the hedge and the buildings and through the kissing gate. Turn right across the narrow field; go through the next kissing gate.
3   Continue ahead on the right hand field edge with the hedge to the right. Go through the gap in the corner and turn left along the left hand field edge. At the top turn right for 130yds, go through the hedge gap and turn right, back to the original direction with the hedge now to the

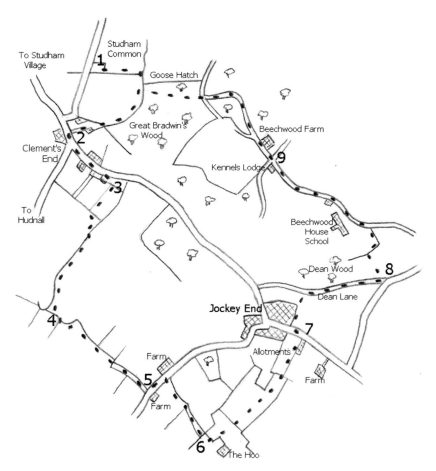

right, bearing left up to the wide gateway.

4 Go through and take the field edge (hedge now left), bearing left into the corner, turn right and keep direction along field edges, through two metal gates and follow the hedged path all the way to the road.

5 Turn left for 300yds to the signpost and turn right up the path between the hedge and the fence. Go straight on at the boundary with the lower fence now right; cross the stile and keep ahead nearly to the outbuildings.

6 Step over the stile on the left and take the path along the short right hand field edge, keep direction across two fields which may be under cultivation, a path however should be visible within any crops. Pass through the kissing gate and continue slight right over the stile in the middle of the fence ahead. Carry on past the overgrown allotments to the road.

7   Turn left for 150yds to the signpost and turn right along the edge of the playing field. Keep direction past the end of the houses, down slope and through the hedge gap. Turn right along Dean Lane, the wide hedged bridleway, all the way to the road.

8   Go through the kissing gate on the left, up the slope of the field and through this kissing gate into the sports field, turn right and with the fence to the road follow the field edge through the trees in the corner to the school access drive. Turn left up the drive, passing right of the school and continue along the hardcore road to the crossroads at Kennels Lodge.

9   Carry on left of Beechwood Farm and bear right, through the trees. Keep straight on past a road to the right, up to the T-junction and keep direction along the narrow path through the trees of Goose Hatch. Exit on to the field edge and turn right, take the path through the gap at the hedge corner and turn left back to the starting point at the car park.

Background Information

Straw plaiting was an important cottage industry in the Chilterns area until the last part of the 19th century. Wheat straw grown on chalk was thought to be the best quality for making hats. Straw was split lengthways with a special cutter and plaited into long strips by women and children. A skilled woman could often earn more than her husband. It was then gathered into bundles and sent off, normally to Luton to make bonnets and straw hats. Business slowed and then ended during the last third of the 19th century, one of the first trades to be devastated by cheap imports from the Far East, coupled with changes in fashion as straw bonnets became far less popular even for agricultural labour.

16 Dunstable Downs

Out along the top of the Downs – return on the footpath at the bottom of the slope.

4½ Miles	**2 Hours**

Location and Parking   Use the car park at the Chilterns Gateway Centre at the top of Dunstable Downs, pay and display.
Grid Reference   TL 007197
Ordnance Survey   Explorer Map nos 181, 182 and 193 (there are small sections on each map), Landranger Map no 165 and 166.
Facilities   Toilets, café and shop in the Visitor Centre.
Start   From the Visitor Centre.
Description   Good paths, some stiles and gates, one steep slope down and the return slope back up to the top of the downs near the end.

The Walk

1   Follow the gravel path from the Visitor Centre down to the ventilation cowling. Turn left past the marker post with the blue arrow along the path between the trees and the fence. Go through the metal gate and ahead past the pylon to the signpost at the corner of the trees.

2   Turn left up the slope with the trees to the right, through this metal gate and up the hardcore path at the edge of the trees. Go across the road and bear right, keep right, past the marker post and join the tarmac driveway ahead. Continue past Chute Farm and bear left with the road.

3   Turn right, through the kissing gate on the right and follow the wide field edge with the hedge to the right. Go through the boundary and the kissing gate, keep direction through the next kissing gate and descend the steps to the sunken path.

4   Take the track right, to the marker post, bear right to the next marker post and turn left down to the bottom of the slope. Turn right through the lower National Trust kissing gate, signposted Whipsnade.

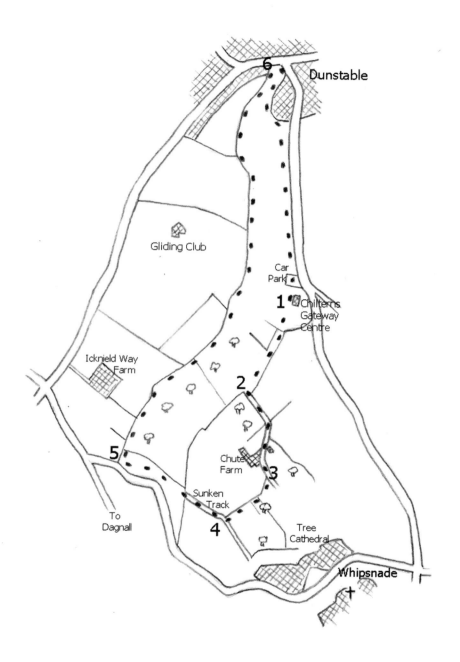

Dunstable

6

Gliding Club

Car
Park

1 Chilterns
Gateway
Centre

Icknield Way
Farm

2

5

Chute
Farm

3

Sunken
Track

To
Dagnall

4

Tree
Cathedral

Whipsnade

59

5 Follow this path along the bottom of the slope all the way to the grassy area close to the B489 road in Dunstable.

6 Turn around and go back up the slope close to the backs of the houses to the left, through a gate and continue along the top of the Downs back to the Chilterns Gateway Centre and the starting point.

Background Information

The junction close to the visitor centre is called Robertson Corner after the memorial placed there by William Robertson in memory of his brothers killed in the First World War. Various pieces of land on the Downs were purchased between 1935 and 1948, the latter parts with the aid of the Robertson legacy. See notes after walk no 37 (Sharpenhoe Clappers).

The London Gliding Club was formed in 1930, members started by launching gliders from the top of Ivinghoe Beacon. This was soon stopped as crowds of spectators disturbed other visitors. The club and the crowds moved to the present site below the Downs.

Gliding first became popular in Germany after the First World War. Powered aircraft had been banned by the Treaty of Versailles and this was a way around it. A competition in 1920 was won by a flight of two kilometres lasting two minutes; by 1930 gliders had flown over 100 miles in one flight.

There is still a strong German influence within the sport, nearly a third of current glider pilots are German.

17 Flitwick Moor

Flitwick – Pulloxhill – Greenfield – Flitwick Moor

5¼ Miles   **2½ Hours**

Location and Parking   Use the car park off Station Road, close to the roundabout in the centre of Flitwick. It is also possible to park in the car park at point **8**; turn on to the hardcore road at Folly Farm and continue to the car park.
Grid Reference   TL035349
Ordnance Survey   Explorer Map no193, Landranger Map nos 153 and 166, (most is on 166).
Facilities   No toilets.   There is a Tesco supermarket close to the station; pubs, shops, cafés and takeaways in the town.
Start   From the car park.
Description   An easy level walk with a few gates and stiles, some short sections could be muddy in wet weather.

The Walk

1   Go back up to Station Road and turn right, away from the town; continue ahead along Water Lane bearing right to the bottom corner. Cross the footbridge and bear right with the stream to the right, up to the marker post.

2   Turn left between the trees and the fence to the next stream and bear right over the substantial footbridge, turn left along the path through the trees to the marker post on the far side. Follow the field edge to a low marker post and turn right, over a sleeper footbridge. Take the hardcore access road to the left, up to the road.

3   Turn left for 80yds along this surprisingly busy road and take the road right, past the cul-de-sac sign. Continue ahead on this track and keep going as the track gets more overgrown. Go past the signpost, maintain direction across the rough grassland past a telegraph pole and carry on upslope along the field edge with the hedge to the right.

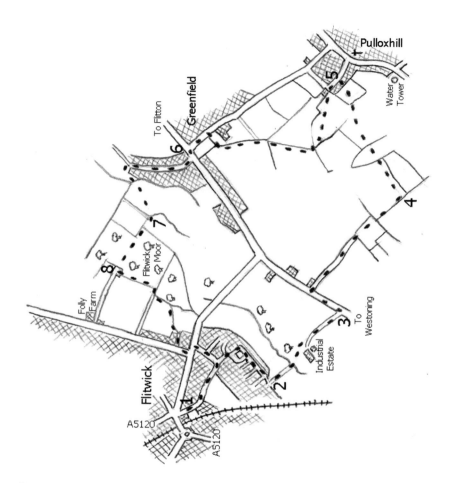

4   At the marker post turn left over the open field, which may be under cultivation although a path should be well marked, to the hedge gap and cross over the footbridge. Continue up the slope ahead with the barbed wire fence to the left. Follow the fence through the dip and over the footbridge at the yellow top marker post. Keep direction (a track should be visible) across the narrow strip of field and step over the stile. Bear right through the gate in the far corner, turn left through the wooden kissing gate and follow the enclosed path between houses to the road.
5   Turn left along the road (Tyburn Lane in Pulloxhill) to the signpost at the corner. Turn left into the field and take a right hand diagonal (a

track should be visible) to the bottom corner. Go through the hedge gap; turn left with the fence to the right and follow the fence to the right down to the boundary. Cross over the three sleeper footbridge and bear right, hedge still right, carry on past the farmyard to the marker disc. Turn right, along the left hand field edge up to the road, cross and take the roadside path to the T-junction.

6   Cross and turn left, take Mill Lane to the right and follow the road between houses past the end to the kissing gate on the left. Turn left and go along the path bearing left at the back of the houses, over the footbridge and through the next kissing gate. Take a diagonal across this part of the moor to the far corner.

7   Go over the footbridge and turn right through the kissing gate in the corner. Continue along the path through the trees to the car park at the far edge of the moor.

8   Turn left along the edge of the trees to the information board and right, up to the marker post at the corner of the trees. Turn left and follow the field edge with the trees to the left, to the edge of Flitwick. Turn left along Moor Lane to the T-junction and left to the main road, keep ahead up Station Road, bearing right to the town centre and the car park.

Background Information

Flitwick Moor is an unusual Site of Special Scientific Interest consisting of acid peat bog and alkaline fen close together. It was formed by reeds, sedges and water based vegetation decaying into the mud and water for several thousands of years. This site is the only survivor of numerous others that existed along the valley of the River Flit. In 2007 the Moor was under threat from a housing development company; thanks to the uproar provoked and the protests of local people this seems to have been averted at the moment.

During the 19th century people were attracted from far away to soak cloths in the water and apply them to diseased or injured parts of the body. They believed that the iron rich water had special healing power. The water was bottled and sold by a company in the early part of the 20th century as a restorative tonic.

As late as the 1960s the peat here was cut and sold commercially for use by gardeners and farmers. It was also used by the provincial and then nationalised gas companies in purification processes.

Nature Notes

The moor is home to a wide range of mammals, birds and insects; there are thought to be over 700 different variations of plants around the site.

18 Golden Valley

Ashridge Park – Northchurch Common – Berkhamsted Common – Ashridge College – Little Gaddesden – Ringshall

7¼ Miles	3½ Hours

Location and Parking Use the car park close to the visitor centre at the Bridgewater Memorial in Ashridge Park. The centre is signposted from the B4506 between Berkhamsted and Dagnall.
Grid Reference SP971131
Ordnance Survey Explorer Map no 181, Landranger Map nos 165/166.
Facilities Toilets, National Trust shop and café in the centre. Picnic area adjacent.
Start At the monument.
Description A fairly level walk through trees, parkland and field edges on good paths. More care should be taken on paths in the trees as they are less distinct and it is far easier to get lost. Some stiles and gates.

The Walk

1 Start away from the monument along the road back towards the entrance for 350yds to the signpost. Turn right along the concrete then narrower dirt path between trees. The track crosses a road after two thirds of a mile; keep direction past a marker post on a fairly indistinct path to a marker post with yellow and blue arrows.
2 Bear right up a wide track to the marker post and take the track left/straight on through less dense tree growth. Continue between open land and trees into the corner and bear left past a marker post.
3 Go along the track with the hedge and the trees to the right, the circle of conifers on the left. Fork right, to the parking area at the road and turn right along the wide grass verge.

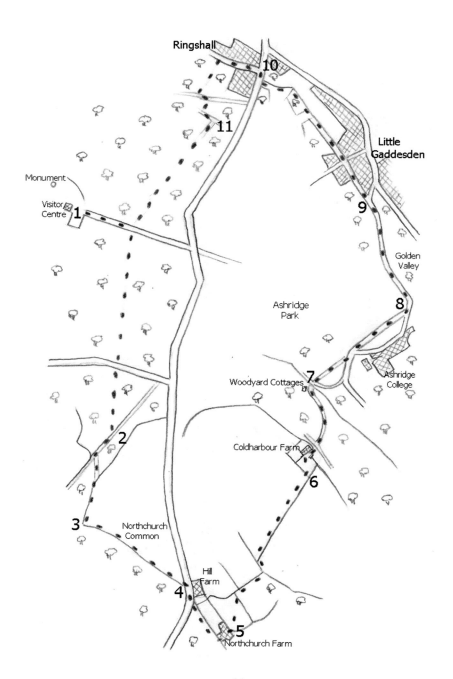

Ringshall

10

11

Little
Gaddesden

Monument

Visitor
Centre
1

9

Golden
Valley

Ashridge
Park

8

7
Woodyard Cottages

Ashridge
College

Coldharbour Farm

6

2

3
Northchurch
Common

Hill
Farm

4

5
Northchurch Farm

4 As the road swings right turn left at the signpost, fork left past the marker post with the red disc and continue for 400yds to the tarmac drive. Turn sharp left and go through the narrow wooden gate next to the Leawood House sign. Keep ahead with Northchurch Farm to the right, on the tarmac then hardcore access road and pass through the metal kissing gate.

5 Bear left across the field, a track should be visible in the grass, to the far corner and go through the gap at the white post. Walk along the field edge ahead, bearing right with the hedge to the left. Go through the narrow wooden gate and down the wide hardcore track. Follow the track left through the next gate and right, uphill with the hedge to the right for half a mile to the stile.

6 Step over the stile and cross the field on a left hand diagonal to the opposite fence, bear right through the narrow gate; continue ahead through the farmyard past Coldharbour Farm and go through the gate. Carry on up the wide hardcore road bearing left and then right past Woodyard Cottages.

7 As this road turns further right take the path ahead through the wooden barriers, uphill with the barbed wire fence and the field to the left and the trees to the right. Keep ahead through the trees and join the road left/straight on, continue on the grass next to the road with Ashridge College to the right.

8 Bear left with the road at the toll hut, carry on further left with Golden Valley now to the right and keep on the road through the trees.

9 Where the road swings right to the park entrance, go straight on up Ringshall Drive and keep ahead as the road becomes a narrower dirt track through the trees. Cross the stile and bear left between the hedge and open ground up to the road.

10 Turn right and immediate left into Beacon Road for 320yds to the footpath signpost. Take the path to the left upslope past a marker post for 450yds to a yellow arrow marker post and turn left for 180yds to the next marker post. Turn right on the wide path for 120yds to another marker post, then left for 320yds to the marked crossroads within sight of the road.

11 Turn right and keep direction past junctions and marker posts to the main driveway. Turn right back to the car park and the visitor centre.

Background Information

Edmund of Almain (1249-1300), was the nephew of King Henry III and the second Earl of Cornwall. Edmund visited Germany in 1268 with his father and obtained a glass phial said to hold some of the blood of Christ; it had reputedly once belonged to Charlemagne. In 1283 he founded Ashridge Priory to look after the relic and pilgrims flocked to see it. The priory became well known and very rich. A parliament was held there in 1290 by King Edward I (Edmund's cousin).

At the Reformation the priory was surrendered to King Henry VIII and it was used by his children. His son Edward VI gave the estate to Princess Elizabeth, the future Elizabeth I. She was arrested here in 1554 and accused of treason.

The priory buildings were used as a home by the Bridgewaters during their ownership. The 3rd Duke having made so much money from mining and canals, decided to demolish the old structure and start again. He unfortunately died before the new house could be started and it was left to the 7th Earl. The present Neo-Gothic mansion was designed by architect James Wyatt and completed in 1813. The gardens were laid out at the same time by Humphry Repton.

The Brownlows who were owners during the latter half of the 19th century were regarded as good landlords by their tenants, but there were however a long list of rules to be obeyed. All bedroom windows in an estate house had to be opened every morning between 8 and 12, no washing could be hung out on Sundays and if a child were judged to be lazy or delinquent the parents would be fined five shillings (25 pence), a fair amount in Victorian times for ordinary people.

The house was bought by businessman Urban Hanlon Broughton and given to a trust established by the Conservative Prime Minister, Andrew Bonar Law (1858-1923). The Conservative Party ran a College of Citizenship there from 1929. During the Second World War the house was used as a hospital and maternity unit; post war it was used for short periods as a teacher training college and a record office. Since 1959 it has been the Ashridge Business School, a respected Management Training College.

Ashridge has been used several times in films. Parts of the Harry Potter series were filmed here and the house was a backdrop to the 1967 film 'The Dirty Dozen'.

19 Totternhoe Knolls

Totternhoe Knolls Nature Reserve – Maiden Bower

---

4 Miles   **2 Hours**

Location and Parking The car park at Totternhoe Knolls, signposted from Castle Hill Road (the main road) in Totternhoe village.
Grid Reference SP986218
Ordnance Survey Explorer Map no 192, Landranger Map no 165.
Facilities Picnic tables only. No toilets. Pubs, the 'Cross Keys' on Castle Hill Road and the 'Old Farm Inn' in Church End.
Start Leave from the car park.
Description Good paths but several slopes, mainly gates, few stiles. The route passes the Castle Mound and Maiden Bower Iron Age site, both worth a detour. The Sewell Greenway Cycleway passes between points **4** and **5**.

The Walk

1   Go out of the front of the car park entrance down to the kissing gate and turn right along the fenced path to the junction. Bear left along the wider hardcore track past the metal barrier; just before the next kissing gate bear right through the trees, curving slight left to the marker post.

2   Turn sharp right down the slope and left at the next corner to a yellow topped marker post on the right. Turn sharper right down the narrow path between the fence and the hedge and follow this path left and right, then left at the factory down to the tarmac road.

3   Take the road right, left of the factory with the brick wall to the right, past the metal barrier to the T-junction of paths next to the marker post. Turn right along the right hand path to the marker post and turn left over the parallel road.

4   Go up the wide byway between hedges past the signpost at the old railway bridge (the Sewell Greenway uses the old railway line) and keep direction uphill to the second signpost near the top of the slope. Bear right still between hedges, with the hill fort Maiden Bower to the right, past a marker post towards the houses of Dunstable.

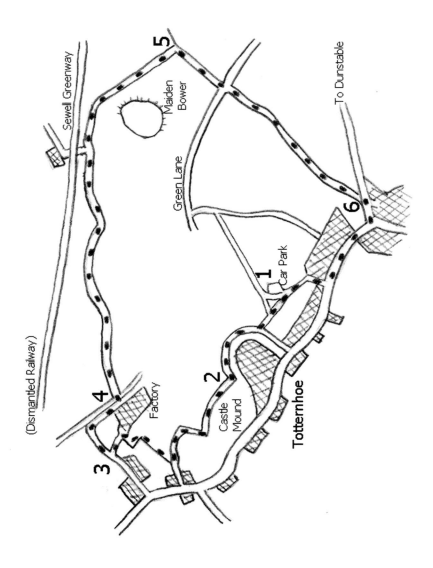

5 Follow the path right at the marker post, go over the crossroads at the wider track and continue downhill past the cricket ground to the road.

6 Turn right along the roadside path to the Totternhoe Knolls signpost and turn right, up the slope to the car park and the starting point.

Background Information

The Maiden Bower Iron Age Fort was built on the site of an earlier Neolithic earthwork. This first rampart appears to have been part of a more complicated structure and was perhaps built as some kind of religious meeting place or burial ground. The Normans also built a castle at Totternhoe but chose the high ground at the northwest end of the village.

The quarries locally have produced a chalk based stone known as Totternhoe Clunch. It is a fairly soft stone and does not weather well, crumbling in wet weather and frost, so has consequently been used mainly inside buildings. The most obvious local use is at Luton Parish Church where the white stone laid alternately with flint blocks to form a chequered pattern. It has also been used at Woburn, Ashridge House and Westminster Abbey.

The factory still produces hydrated lime; the stone is not quarried locally but brought in from other parts of the country. There was once a far bigger local industry producing cement, gypsum and agricultural lime.

Nature Notes

Totternhoe Knolls nature reserve is a stronghold of the Small Blue, at only one inch or 25mm wide it is Britain's smallest butterfly. It is in spite of its name not particularly blue; the top is bluish brown and the underside grey with a silvery tinge and small black spots. It is a resident of man made habitats, particularly disused quarries and gravel pits, eating only the flowers of the kidney vetch plant which thrives in these situations. The female lays eggs no bigger than a pinhead on the yellow flowers of these plants and the caterpillars feed on the seeds before digging into the soil to form the chrysalis, emerging as a butterfly the next spring.

20 Aylesbury Arm

Startop's End – Marsworth Top Lock – Tring Wharf – Little Tring – Wilstone Reservoir – Aylesbury Arm

---

6¼ Miles   3 Hours

Location and Parking Use the car park (pay and display) at Marsworth off the B489 between the grand Union Canal and Startop's end Reservoir. An alternative parking site is the Wilstone Reservoir car park on the B489 close to point **7**.

Grid Reference SP920141

Ordnance Survey Explorer Map no 181, Landranger Map no 165.

Facilities No toilets; café adjacent and pub the 'Anglers Retreat' on the canal's edge on the other side of the B489.

Start From the car park.

Description The route is mainly on canal towpaths and field edges with some gates and stiles. Fairly level with some slight slopes. The walk uses a busy section of road between the Wilstone reservoir car park and point **7**.

The Walk

1 Leave through the gate at the far end of the car park, along the path with the canal to the left, past the locks and over the footbridge at Marsworth Top Lock.

2 Turn left at the bottom to take the path to the right, along the left hand side of the Wendover Arm branch of the canal. At the road, cross the bridge and continue with the canal now to the left, past the mill, all the way to the next bridge (no 3).

3 Cross the road, go down the wooden steps and take the path ahead between the canal and the barbed wire fence (the canal is on the right again). At the marker post bear left between fences, go through the gate and continue ahead to the stile in the far corner. Step over and keep the original direction with the fence now left, bearing left and cross the stile ahead.

4 Turn right, up the wide hedged path, through the broken wooden kissing gate and continue downhill. Cross the footbridge over the dry canal and turn right along the towpath to the marker post. Take the steps down to the left and go along the right hand field edge with the fence to the right, follow the boundary left in the corner.

5 Go through the boundary and turn right, the path crosses the field

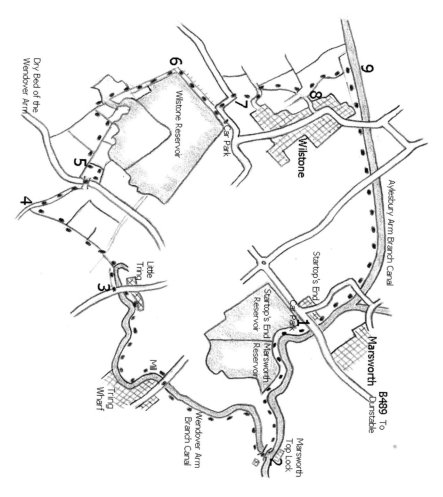

on a diagonal to the opposite corner but it is often easier to take the path around the edge of the field. Turn right on the track along the right hand field edge with the trees to the right over the footbridge/stile in the hedge gap ahead. Bear left across the corner of the field to the stile, do not cross; turn right over to the opposite corner (the right hand field edge is often used as a more direct, but unofficial path). Take the enclosed path through the boundary, then ahead with Wilstone Reservoir to the right.

6   Turn right at the reservoir corner along the embankment and go down the steps to the car park. Leave by the exit and turn left/ahead up this narrow section of busy road to the corner and turn right over the crash barrier, the footbridge and the stiles.

7   Bear right across the field to the far corner, step over the stile and turn right then left along the wide farm road. Cross the stile next to the wide metal gate and go down the short length of fenced path, turn right along the field edge with the stream and the trees to the right. Go over the stile and keep ahead to the marker post.

8   Turn left still in the same field and walk up the field edge with the trees to the right. Bear right where the hedge juts out and cross the footbridge/stile at the sluice on the right. Follow the path left to the Aylesbury Arm branch of the Grand Union Canal.

9   Turn right along the towpath with the canal to the left all the way to the main Grand Union Canal and turn right on this towpath leading back to the car park at Startop's End Reservoir.

Background Information

The importance of an adequate water supply to a canal cannot be overestimated. The highest point or summit level needs to be as long as possible to hold as much water as it can and act as its own reservoir, as regular traffic on a busy canal causes a constant drain of water from this section. A barge travelling down from the 370ft high, two and a half mile long, Tring summit level on the Grand Union canal takes over 50,000 gallons of water with it every time a lock is used. This water has to be continually replenished for boats to continue to use the waterway.

The best method of doing this is to build the canal so that it has a stream or natural source of water flowing directly into it. This system had its drawbacks as the canal companies often had to agree to limits on the amount of water they used or arrange to return the same amount of water further down the watercourse.

Some canals were built with large stationary steam engines to pump the water from lower canal levels back to a higher point so that the water could effectively be used at least twice. The most popular method used by canal engineers was to build conveniently sited reservoirs to supply water as and when needed directly into the canal.

The Wendover Arm of the Grand Junction Canal was completed in 1797. It was originally planned as just a narrow feeder canal taking water from streams around Wendover, directly into the summit level of the main canal between Bulbourne and Cow Roast Locks. It had quickly been realised that it could cheaply and easily be made into a navigable canal. The canal unfortunately always lost a great deal of water, so in 1802 a reservoir was built at Wilstone to prevent excess water being lost. The other three reservoirs were built between 1806 and 1817; a steam powered beam engine was installed in 1818 to pump water into the reservoir.

By the mid 19th century the Wendover Arm was leaking a million gallons of water each day; several unsuccessful attempts were made to cure this problem. At the end of the century the Arm was actually taking water from the main canal. In 1904 most of the Arm was drained and a pipeline laid under the bed of the Canal.

The Wendover Arm Trust, a voluntary organisation set up in 1989, is endeavouring to restore the canal to its former glory along the complete route. Some of the ongoing restoration can be seen west of Little Tring where the canal presently ends.

The Aylesbury Arm although authorised in 1794 was not completed until 1815.

Nature Notes

The reservoirs have always attracted a tremendous variety of wildlife, particularly waterfowl. They were made National Nature Reserves in 1955 and Sites of Special Scientific Interest in 1987.

21 Wilstone Reservoir

Wilstone – Grand Union Canal – Wilstone Reservoir

4 Miles   2 Hours

Location and Parking Use the car park on the B489 at the corner of Wilstone Reservoir close to the turn for Wilstone village.
Grid Reference SP904135
Ordnance Survey Explorer Map no 181, Landranger Map no 165.
Facilities None.
Start From the car park.
Description Very easy short walk, well marked and easy to follow. The route uses canal towpaths, field edges and good paths, one short section over a field can be very muddy in wet weather.

The Walk

1   Go out of the entrance end of the car park along the path at the bottom of the embankment. At the hedge gap, turn left across the road and go through the kissing gate. Take a right hand diagonal over the field to the far corner; keep direction over two footbridges and through three gates to the road. Turn right, to the footpath signpost on the immediate left.

2   Pass through the kissing gate and bear left, go through both kissing gates at the top left of the field and carry on along the road into Wilstone village. Keep ahead past the War Memorial and the 'Half Moon' pub. Follow the road right and turn left at the signpost by the information board. Keep direction on this potholed track to the canal and turn left.

3   Follow the towpath with the canal to the right for two thirds of a mile to the signpost just before lock number 10. Turn left along the field edge with the hedge to the left and keep direction roughly parallel with the telegraph poles all the way to the road.

4   Cross and continue direction over the field which may be under cultivation although a path should be well marked within any crop. At the corner of Wilstone Reservoir turn left through the hedge gap, then right along the top of the embankment with the reservoir to the left.

5 Bear right at the far end into the field, the path from here bears right, to the far side of the field then back to the left into the corner ahead, the path directly ahead along the left hand field edge seems to be the one that is most often used. Cross the stile/footbridge in the corner and carry on up the left hand field edge. Turn left and right to the marker post, then left and right, up the slope to the towpath at the

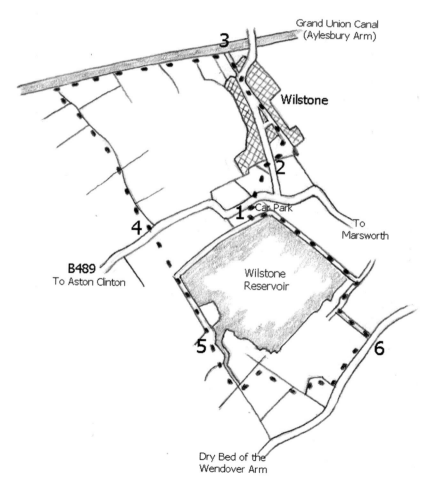

side of the dry bed of the Wendover Arm of the Grand Union Canal. Take the tow path to the left.

6 Just past the wooden footbridge (number 4), turn left at the marker post down to the T-junction. Turn right to the next junction and take the path left along the top of the embankment to the car park at the starting point.

Background Information

The path from the Grand Union Canal to the left hand turn just beyond point 5 is the border between Buckinghamshire and Hertfordshire.

22 Startop's End

Wilstone Reservoir – Wendover Arm – Tringford Reservoir – Grand Union Canal – Startop's End – Aylesbury Arm – Wilstone

---

4 Miles   2 Hours

Location and Parking   Use the car park on the B489 at the corner of Wilstone reservoir close to the turn for Wilstone village. Can also be started from Marsworth at the car park next to the canal at Startop's End Reservoir, (pay and display).
Grid Reference   SP904135
Ordnance Survey   Explorer Map no 181, Landranger Map no 165.
Facilities   None.
Start   From the car park.
Description   Another easy level walk on field edges, good paths and canal towpaths. One short section across a field can be muddy.

The Walk

1   Go up the steps to the top of the embankment and turn left, turn right at the corner and continue to the far corner. Carry on with the trees to the right and follow the path right, to the T-junction. Take the path left up to the towpath next to the dry bed of the Wendover Arm of the Grand Union Canal.

2   Turn left, follow the towpath to the road and take the road to the right to the entrance to Tringford Pumping Station. Double back along the path upslope between the hedge and the fence and turn right, down to the signpost.

3   Turn sharp left on the path left of Tringford Reservoir, keep on the path and bear right, along the water's edge to the road. Turn right along the roadside path to the signpost on the left.

4   Double back beneath the road, past the fishery information board

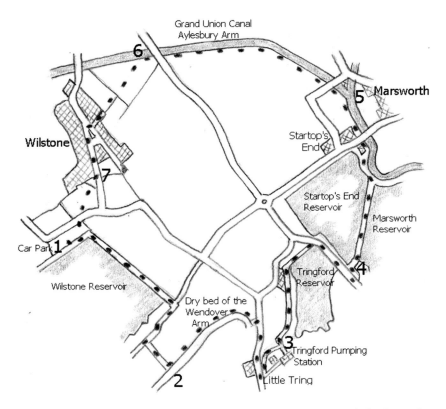

and continue along the path between the reservoirs. Turn left along the towpath with the Grand Union canal to the right through Startop's End; past Marsworth Lock, under the road and right of the 'White Lion'.

5   Follow the towpath left with the Aylesbury Arm now right and carry on for just over half a mile, go under bridge number 2 and up to the signpost on the left (before lock number 7).

6   Turn left through the hedge gap and take a right hand diagonal over the field, which may be under cultivation although a path should be visible within any crop. Go through the hedge gap and follow the left hand field edge, continue ahead to the road in Wilstone village. Walk past the War Memorial and turn left along the roadside path to the signpost on the right.

7   Turn right, through three gates and over two footbridges; keep direction to the kissing gate. Cross the road and turn right along the path to the starting point in the car park.

23 Telegraph Hill

Pegsdon – Hexton – Icknield Way – Telegraph Hill

5¼ Miles   **2¼ Hours**

Location and Parking Pegsdon is on the B655 between Hitchin and Barton-le-Clay; there is sometimes space at the side of the road in this small settlement and also often space at the junction of the B655 and the minor road to Shillington. The walk can also easily be started from Hexton village between points **3** and **4**.
Grid Reference TL118302
Ordnance Survey Explorer Map no 193, Landranger Map no 166.
Facilities No toilets. Pub, the 'Live and Let Live' in the village.
Start At the junction of the B655 and the Shillington road.
Description An easy walk on good paths, some stiles and gates, two stiff slopes to climb and a significant slope down to the finish.

The Walk

1 Take the road away from the B655, past Pegsdon Way and the signpost by the telephone box. Carry on past the derestriction signposts for 400yds and turn left into the cul-de-sac.
2 Keep direction, past the signpost, along the bridlepath with the hedge to the left. Bear right with the track to the signpost, take the path to the left and keep right through the hedge line, past the marker post and the house along tarmac topped Mill Lane.
3 Follow the road left at a junction with a hardcore farm track, continue into Hexton village and keep ahead past the 'Raven' to the B655.
4 Cross and carry on ahead, towards Lilley, for 190yds to the signpost and bear right past the metal gate up the wide hardcore farm track. Carry on ahead, as the track turns right, on the wide grass path uphill through the trees. Continue with the trees to the right, go through the hedge gap and turn right, up to the corner. Take the track to the left along the field edge upslope with the hedge to the right, all the way to

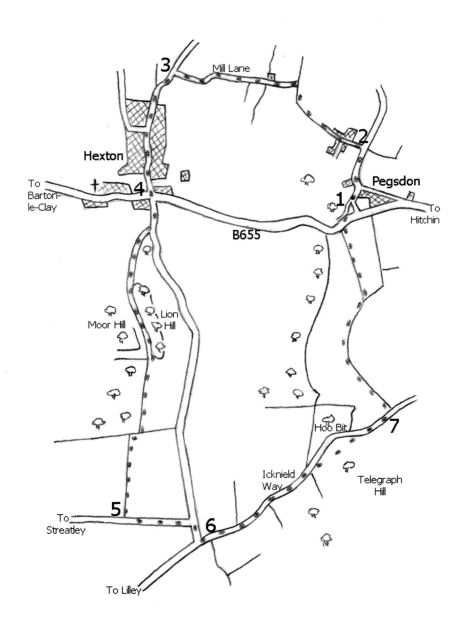

Mill Lane

3

Hexton

To
Barton-
le-Clay

4

2

Pegsdon

1

To
Hitchin

B655

Moor Hill

Lion
Hill

Hoo Bit

7

Icknield
Way

Telegraph
Hill

5

To
Streatley

6

To Lilley

the road.

5 Turn left carefully along the side and the grass verge of this surprisingly busy road, down to the T-junction. Turn right down to the corner at the Icknield Way signposts and turn left past the gate and the barriers.

6 Continue up the slight slope of this substantial path to the Telegraph Hill information board and marker discs. Take the path uphill to the right, up the wide grass path through the trees with Telegraph Hill to the right. Keep ahead along the left hand field edge with the hedge and trees to the left bearing left into the corner. Bear left through the gap and rejoin what has been the parallel track; turn right for 90yds to the marker post on the left.

7 Turn left through the wooden kissing gate and continue ahead with the hedge and the steep slope to the right; there is a viewpoint with a seat just after the hedge starts. Carry on downhill on the obvious track to the B655, Pegsdon and the starting point are on the other side of the road.

Background Information

Telegraph Hill and Ivinghoe Beacon were the sites of beacons during the Elizabethan era to warn people of danger or possible invasion by the Spanish, a real concern to ordinary people during the time of the Spanish Armada. The beacon was not a bonfire but a container of pitch which would burn for hours once set alight. Ivinghoe Beacon could be easily seen from Telegraph Hill. Both had probably been used for many years as signalling stations with their good communications because of their proximity to the Ridgeway National Trail and the Icknield Way. The name is popular in England, several other locations are known as Telegraph Hill.

There is evidence on the slopes between the Icknield Way and Pegsdon of ancient agriculture, terraces called strip lynchets where crops have been grown. There are also signs that minerals have been extracted from small quarry sites around the hill.

Nature Notes

The Chalkhill Blue butterfly is a native of chalk downlands and a common sight on Telegraph Hill from July to September. The male's wings are silvery blue with white outer and black inner edging; females are an all over brown and difficult to identify from several other species, particularly while on the wing.

Hoo Bit, a meadow next to the Icknield Way, is covered in a blaze of wild flowers each springtime.

24 Berkhamsted Common

Nettleden – St Margaret's – Little Gaddesden – Ashridge College – Berkhamsted Common

7 Miles	**3½ Hours**

Location and Parking   Use the car park at Berkhamsted Common opposite the War Memorial, on the road to Ashridge College.
Grid Reference   TL005093
Ordnance Survey   Explorer Map nos 181 and 182, only a very small part is on map no 182; Landranger Map nos 165 and 166.
Facilities   None. Parking only.
Start   From the car park.
Description   A slightly tougher walk, several hefty slopes and a section between points **5** and **6** which could be muddy in wet weather. Apart from this one section the paths are good and well marked, even through the trees in Ashridge Park.

The Walk

1   Cross the road and take the track right of the memorial, be careful as the track immediately crosses a golf course fairway; watch out for golfers driving from the right. Go over a path and fork left on a wide track through the trees, over another fairway. Keep direction into the trees at the edge of the golf course and carry on down to the road.
2   Turn left for 30yds to the signpost and take the narrow path left to the wooden barrier. Go up the hedged path to the right, cross this road and keep ahead on the wider path to the next road in Frithsden.
3   Cross and continue ahead uphill on the tarmac then hardcore permissive bridleway. Carry on downhill between flint and brick walls, under the bridge to the road in Nettleden. Turn left and immediate right at the signpost, uphill on the right hand field edge; cross the stile at the summit and go downhill through the trees to the road in St. Margaret's.

4 Take the tarmac road to the left and continue on the narrower hardcore road through trees for two thirds of a mile to the signpost on the left where the houses start again.

5 Turn left up the edge jutting out and carry on ahead across the field, which may be under cultivation although a path should be well marked within any crop. The path passes right of the small stand of trees and bears right to the narrow kissing gate in the fence. Cross the grass field on a diagonal to the top corner and exit over the stile.

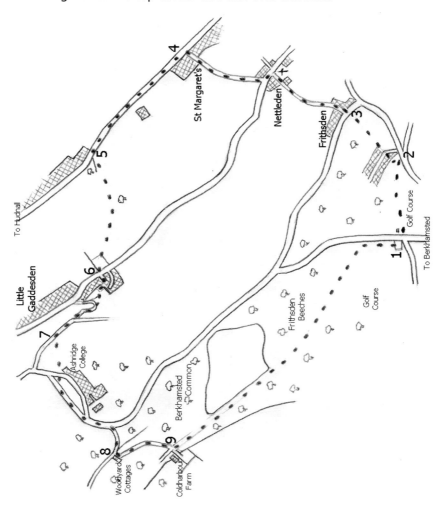

6 Cross the road and keep direction along Cromer Close and the hedged path to the Hertfordshire Way signpost. Turn right along the path between the backs of the houses and bear left through the playing area. Enter the Ashridge estate through the hedge gap and bear right downhill to the semi circle of estate road. Continue downhill on the lower arm, bear left to the marker post and join the estate road to the right.

7 After 150yds take the path bearing left upslope past a marker post and ahead through trees, keep ahead with the fence to the left to the further road and turn left past the front of Ashridge College. Follow the road left into the trees, as the road turns further left fork right towards Woodyard and Coldharbour. Keep on the track right, into the dip past Woodyard Cottages and bear left on a now hardcore road to Coldharbour Farm.

8 Turn left at the bridleway signpost before the gate, past the wooden posts, down a slight slope. After 200yds fork right at a marker post and keep direction on this path, past marker posts, signposts and the golf course for just over a mile. Close to the road the path veers right and parallel to the road leads back to the parking area and the starting point.

Background Information

Berkhamsted Common was the location right through the First World War until 1919, of the Officer Training Camp of the 'Inns of Court' Regiment. The regiment was originally part of the Territorial Army, consisting of men connected to the Law Courts in London. The men referred to themselves as the 'Devil's Own'. Over 14,000 men passed through the camp during the war years; exercises, manoeuvres and mock battles were held each week. The men dug nearly eight miles of trenches on the common to simulate the terrible conditions on the Western Front. The War Memorial opposite the car park is to the 2147 men from the camp killed during the conflict.

25 Doolittle Mill

Totternhoe – Dunstable Downs – Doolittle Mill

6 Miles   3 Hours

Location and Parking   The car park at Totternhoe Knolls, signposted from Castle Hill Road (the main road) in Totternhoe village.
Grid Reference   SP986218
Ordnance Survey   Explorer Map nos 192 and 193, Landranger Map nos 165 and 166.
Facilities   Picnic tables only. No toilets. Pubs, the 'Cross Keys' on Castle Hill Road and the 'Old Farm Inn' in Church End.
Start   Leave from the car park.
Description   Few stiles or gates, good paths and tracks with only one noticeable slope in Totternhoe close to the end of the walk.

The Walk

1   Go through the fence gap at the back of the car park and bear left up the steps, through the narrower fence gap and turn right. Turn almost immediate right uphill on the wide byway. *The Whipsnade White Lion chalk figure can be seen on the hillside off to the right.* At the bottom of the slope bear left past the marker post.
2   Turn right up the wide grass byway, Green Lane and carry on ahead all the way to the B489 in Dunstable. Although the second half of this byway runs between houses it is still a haven of peace and full of wildlife.
3   Cross this busy road right of the roundabout to the grassy area on the corner by the information board. Bear right away from the road close to the trees to the right, past the marker post and up the narrower fenced track through the trees across the slope of the downs. Pass through the kissing gate and bear right past the first marker post to the marker post at the corner of the London Gliding Club.

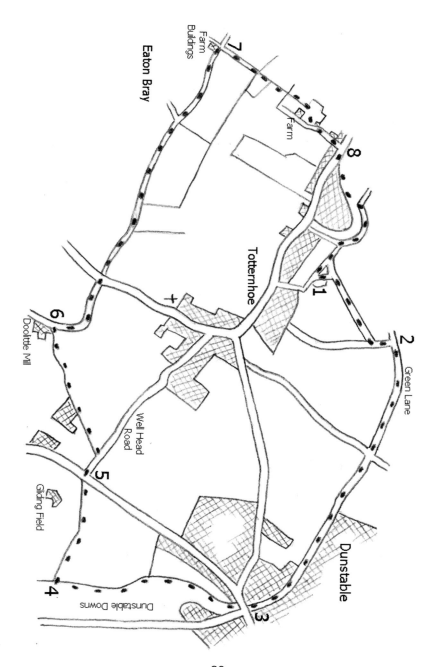

4 Turn right, through the narrow gate, down the path at the edge of the landing field back to the A489.

5 Cross carefully and continue ahead along Wellhead Road to the signpost on the left, go through the narrow gate and continue along the bridleway parallel to the telegraph poles all the way to the road at Doolittle Mill.

6 Turn right and follow the road left at the corner up to the T-junction, keep ahead along the bridleway between the fence and the hedge. Continue ahead for close to a mile, past the first marker post, past the junction with a substantial track to the left and up to the crossroads of paths by the farm buildings.

7 Take the track to the right between the field and the hedge; carry on over the crossroads of paths, between hedges and step over the stile. Keep direction on the left hand, then the right hand field edge. Cross the footbridge and bear right through the orchard and cross the stile in the far corner. Take the narrow tarmac road left up to the main road in Totternhoe.

8 Turn right along the roadside path, past the first signpost and the 'Cross Keys' to the second signpost close to the bus stop. Follow the track up the slope at the back of the houses, through the narrow fence gap and turn right along the stony hardcore bridleway. Fork right between the trees and the fenced open field, go through the kissing gate and turn left back to the car park.

Background Information

Doolittle Mill consists of the remains of both a wind and a watermill. The name was often given to the mill at the top of a stream which was more at the mercy of dry weather and the windmill would certainly have alleviated this potential problem.

The figure of the White Lion on the hillside below Whipsnade Zoo was cut in 1933, to advertise the location of the zoo. At nearly 500ft wide it is thought to be the largest hillside figure in this country.

There are over fifty other figures cut into hillsides in this country, over fifty more have been known to be lost due to a lack of maintenance; vegetation soon grows back if they are untended.

The cutting of figures on chalk hillsides goes back into prehistory, mainly horses and mainly in the south west, particularly Wiltshire. The oldest surviving is the White Horse at Uffington in Oxfordshire; tests have dated the work to between 1400 and 600BC. The newest was completed at Folkestone, Kent in 2003.

The cutting of horses into turf has been called leucippotomy, if it is a human figure like the Cerne Abbas giant it is called gigantotomy; if the cutting of lions does not have a name it could possibly be leopotomy. Technically the figures are called geoglyphs.

26 Bow Brickhill Heath

Woodland on the Woburn Estate

5½ Miles   2¾ Hours

Location and Parking Bow Brickhill is west of the A5, south of Milton Keynes. Find a parking space off Church Road in the trees above the village. There is sometimes room to park near the church.
Grid Reference SP911345
Ordnance Survey Explorer Map no 192, Landranger Map no 165.
Facilities None.
Start From the church.
Description Several slopes to climb, few gates or stiles. Paths are good and in general well marked but it is far easier of course to get lost within trees than open countryside.

The Walk

1 Walk back down the slope towards the village for 160yds to the signpost and turn right, through the gate. Take the track sharp right, up the immediate slope past the top of the steps and keep direction on a fairly indistinct path leading to a more substantial path at a junction. (This is the most difficult part of the walk, if the track is lost continue ahead to the path at the nearest point and turn right).

2 Turn right along this wider path and carry on to the road at a junction, (another, wider track comes in from the left here). Take the tarmac road left, down to the signpost on the right and go through the barrier. Walk up the field edge with the trees to the right, to the marker post at the top.

3 Turn left on the wide track through the edge of the trees to the marker post at the end; take the woodchip path to the right which then becomes a hardcore surface. Go past a marker post and over a wider path; continue ahead on the narrower track through the trees to the road.

4 Turn right and immediate left past signposts and a metal gate, at

92

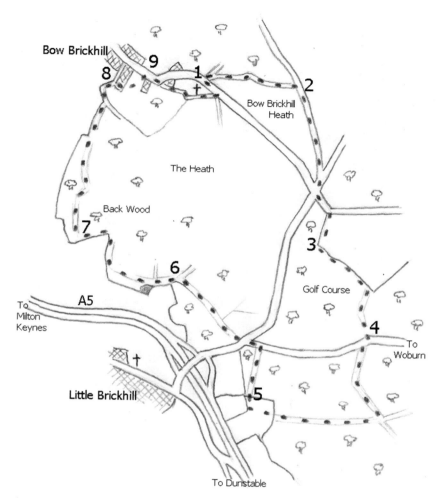

the marker post in the trees take the path to the left. Turn right after nearly half a mile, at the second marker post on a crossroads of paths. Follow this path, fork right, keeping to the narrower path; turn right and immediate left at a forest road to keep direction to the end and exit over a stile in the fence. Cross the field ahead and turn right in front of the stile, up to the stile in the corner.

5 Keep direction through trees again, up to the road; turn left for 90yds to the bridleway signpost at the junction. Turn right through the narrow gate and bear left on the path downhill through the undergrowth.

At the junction at the bottom, turn left along the edge of the trees; go past the pond and keep on this path to a junction of paths.

6 Take the path sharp left and fork left up to a marker post; turn right, still through trees. Continue left/straight on at the corner of a more substantial track and keep direction to the edge of Bow Brickhill village.

7 Just past the yellow bollard, turn right at the signpost uphill between the fence and the hedge. Cross the stile above the sleepers and follow the path on a diagonal over a narrow footbridge to the top corner left of the row of white cottages.

8 Step over the stile on to the road and turn right. Keep straight on along the signposted byway, past the gate, still upslope right of the church, back to the road and the starting point at the parking area.

Background Information

The Greensand Ridge Walk, just touched by this walk between points **4** and **5**, is a forty mile recreational path between Leighton Buzzard and Gamblingay in Cambridgeshire, first opened in 1986. It is a popular route on good paths, well signposted with its silhouette logo of a Muntjac Deer.

27 Goose Hatch

Markyate – Kensworth – Holywell – Studham – Studham Common – Roe End

---

7 Miles   **3½ Hours**

Location and Parking   Markyate is on the A5 trunk road, south east of Dunstable at the junction of the B4540 from Luton. There is a small car park on Hicks Road, between the village centre and the A5.
Grid Reference   TL062164
Ordnance Survey   Explorer Map no 182. Landranger Map nos 165/166.
Facilities   No toilets. Shops, pubs and other facilities all close by in the village.
Start   The crossroads in the centre of the village
Description   An easy walk with some stiles and gates; good, well marked paths and few slopes.

The Walk

1   Leave North West along the High Street to Cavendish Road (close to the 'Red Lion'). Turn left upslope for 280yds to the footpath signpost and turn right along the path between hedges passing right of the village hall. Keep on the right hand side of the playing fields hedges to the right, go through the gap in the corner and continue on the field edge with the hedge still right.
2   Walk through the wide gap at the end and bear left over the corner of the field which may be under cultivation although a path should be well marked within any crop. Go through the narrow gap marked by a yellow topped post, bear right across the field (a track should be visible) to the right hand corner of the trees ahead. Keep direction past the wood and carry on over the next section of field.
3   Pass through the metal kissing gate and continue with the hedge to the left, towards the far corner. At an unmarked point, bear right across

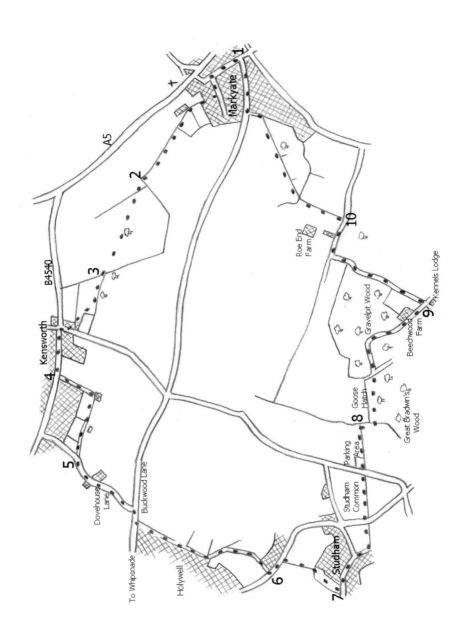

the field and go through the metal gate under a crude metal frame. Keep direction over the field corner, out of the gate and along the gravel drive to the road in Kensworth village. Turn right to the crossroads and left along Common Road to the signpost at the end of the driveway.

4 Turn left through the narrow white pinch stile marked by a yellow disc up the driveway and bear right at the yellow top post, keeping direction up the narrow hedged path parallel to the drive. Follow this path as it swings right, between the hedge and the fence, then through trees. Carry on along the track and the wider hardcore access road to Dovehouse lane at a corner.

5 Continue left/straight on, through the dip and carry on to the T-junction at Buckwood Lane. Turn right for 85yds to the signpost; take the track to the left and fork left at the marker post up the path through the trees with the houses to the right. Keep direction on the field edge and between the fences and the trees, follow the path left between fences and down through the trees to the road.

6 Turn left for 160yds and right through the kissing gate, uphill on the right hand field edge with the trees to the right. Keep ahead past the first marker post and step over the stile at the second marker post; bear right up the wide fenced path to the road.

7 Follow the road left into Studham village, down to the corner and turn right, towards the school. At the bottom turn left onto Studham Common and bear right on the path through the trees on the right hand edge of the common. Keep ahead over the road and the footbridge; maintain direction still on the right hand edge of the now open common, with the trees to the right. Continue over the next road through the parking area to the boundary at the far corner.

8 Turn right, through the gap and up the field edge with the trees to the left for 180yds to the signpost. Turn left between the gateposts, through the trees of Goose Hatch. At the signpost keep direction along the more substantial track bearing right then left, passing right of Beechwood Farm.

9 At the three way signpost on the junction next to Kennels Lodge, turn left and carry on along the road. Continue through the dip and up the slope to the signpost at Roe End Lane. Turn right up the narrow tarmac road past Roe End Farm to the signpost.

10 Turn left through the kissing gate and go up the field edge to the far corner. Bear right through the gap along the grass path between fields, and continue with the hedge and the trees to the right all the way to the road. Take the road right, back into Markyate and the starting point.

Background Information

The legend of the 'Wicked Lady', a female highwayman of the 17th century, has its origins at Markyate Cell. The Cell is a country house built on the site of a 12th century Benedictine Priory founded by the nun Christina of Markyate. The legend tells of a daughter of the house, Lady Katherine Ferrers (1634-1660), who actually existed but that is all that is known about her. She is reputed to have become a highwaywoman after she was forced into marriage and her inheritance frittered away by her father-in-law during the Civil War. She supposedly teamed up with an accomplice Ralph Chaplin, they terrorised Nomansland Common for some time before a robbery went badly wrong. Chaplin was caught and later hanged; Katherine shot and badly wounded. She managed to get to the gates of her house but died there; her body was picked up by loyal servants and spirited away for burial. The legend has been fuelled by the 1945 and 1983 films, the first was very popular, the second bombed badly at the box office.

In reality Katherine Ferrers' stepfather, Simon Fanshawe married her off to his nephew Thomas Fanshawe in 1648 (Simon did then sell off a lot of her property). Markyate Cell was sold in 1657 so it couldn't have been the scene of her death. Nomansland Common is a long way from Markyate (about a mile south of Wheathampstead) to travel for a night's thieving and get back again by dawn. There is no record of Ralph Chaplin ever existing. Records do confirm that Lady Katherine Fanshawe died in 1660 and was buried on 13th June 1660 in Ware on the other side of Hertfordshire. A young woman dying at 26 was not unusual in those days; it may have been in childbirth or any number of other causes.

Stories of women dressing up as pirates, soldiers and highwaymen have always been popular; this is possibly a story that sounded good at the first telling and has aged well.

28 Lilley Hoo

Wellbury – Summer Wood – Lilley Hoo – Telegraph Hill – Icknield Way

5 Miles   **2 Hours**

Location and Parking Use the small parking area on the south side of the B655 between Hitchin and Barton-le-Clay, the left hand side approaching from the Hitchin Direction. This is easily missed and please be wary of fast moving traffic when manoeuvring on this road.
Grid Reference TL132300
Ordnance Survey Explorer Map no 193, Landranger Map no 166.
Facilities None.
Start From the parking area.
Description Good paths with a few gates and easy gentle slopes. Countryside only, no villages on the route.

The Walk

1 Leave the parking area to the right along the road in the Hitchin direction. Walk along the wide grass verge for 400yds, turn right at the signpost for New Wellbury Farm and follow this farm road up the slight slope to the junction.
2 Bear right, along the potholed hardcore road as it bears left past Markham's Lodge and continue uphill. The road bears right past Summer Wood to a junction at a white house (South Lodge), carry on ahead and keep straight on at the crossroads of tracks at the marker post.
3 Continue direction through the wide gap left of the wood, Newfield Spring and carry on down the grass track between fields. Bear left with the hedge to the left, parallel to the telegraph poles. The track veers right downslope until it is parallel with the A505; go past the gate and on to tarmac Lilleyhoo Lane.
4 Turn right and keep ahead uphill past two marker posts and through the hedge gap to the third marker post. Take the track left/ahead between fields along Lilly Hoo; keep direction with the trees to the right

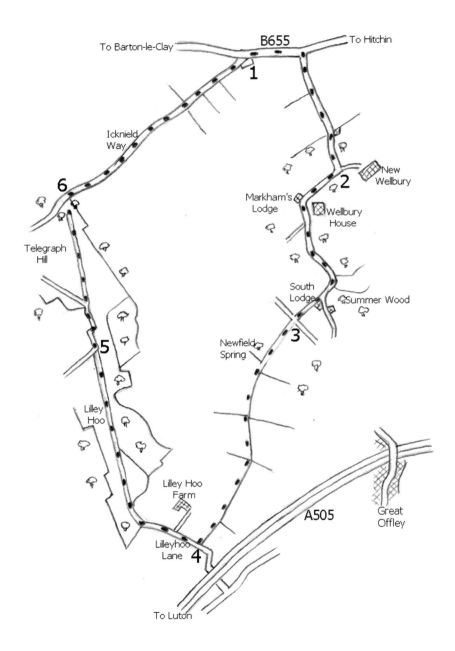

To Barton-le-Clay
B655
To Hitchin

1

Icknield Way

6

New Wellbury

2

Markham's Lodge

Wellbury House

Telegraph Hill

South Lodge

Summer Wood

5

Newfield Spring

3

Lilley Hoo

Lilley Hoo Farm

A505

Great Offley

Lilleyhoo Lane
4

To Luton

and then up to the corner.

5 Continue on the farm road with the hedge now left around the corners, at the fork bear right/ahead on the track across the field. Carry on along the path through the trees right of Telegraph Hill to the junction with the Icknield Way.

6 Turn right and follow this substantial path down to the car park and the starting point.

<u>Nature Notes</u>

Look out for Buzzards, a bird of prey which seems to be increasing its presence in the area. A large bird with a wingspan of about four feet, it can often be seen soaring in thermals, sometimes two or three birds together calling to one another as they search for prey (rabbits and small mammals) or carrion. They may also perch motionless on telegraph poles or posts waiting and watching. The birds are slightly smaller than the Red Kite; they do not have the characteristic forked tail of the kite and are varying shades of brown rather than red.

29 Whistle Brook

Cheddington – Whistle Brook – Horton

5¼ Miles   2¾ Hours

Location and Parking Cheddington is on a minor road parallel to the A488, north west of Pitstone. There is sometimes space in the village hall car park at the south end of the village.
Grid Reference SP923174
Ordnance Survey Explorer Map no 181, Landranger Map no 165.
Facilities No toilets. Local pubs the 'Old Swan' and the 'Three Horseshoes'.
Start From The Green.
Description A level walk with a few gates and stiles on an easy to follow route. The walk uses the grass verge of the busy B488 between points **2** and **3**. Be very careful from point **6** walking through Horton village as the road is busy and quite narrow with no path.

The Walk
1   Take the High Street south, towards Pitstone and turn left at the signpost between numbers 37 and 39. Cross the stile on the right and bear left on the left hand field edge, carry on through the arch of the railway bridge.
2   Keep ahead over the field, up the field edge with the hedge to the right. Follow this right hand field edge to the road; turn right carefully along the grass verge of this surprisingly busy road, over the canal and up to the signpost on the left.
3   Turn left through the metal gate and walk up the farm road with the hedge to the right. At the top turn left at the marker post then right over the stile. Turn left through the gate and cross the footbridge over Whistle Brook; turn immediate right over the adjacent stile/footbridge.
4   Continue ahead, hedge still to the right. At the third boundary, (where the wires cross overhead), bear left and cross the footbridge/ stiles ahead. Bear further left through the wide gate, keep direction

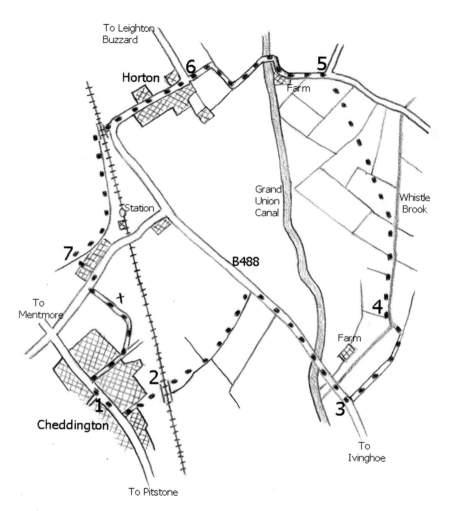

To Leighton Buzzard

Horton

6

5

Farm

Grand Union Canal

Whistle Brook

Station

7

B488

To Mentmore

4

Farm

2

1

3

Cheddington

To Ivinghoe

To Pitstone

and go through the metal kissing gate and footbridge in the hedge. Continue direction through the next gateway to the road.

5 Turn left, past the cul-de-sac sign to the farmhouse and bear right to the canal. Keep ahead along the wide grass track; follow the track right in the corner and left up to the corner in Horton village.

6 Continue ahead through the village; be very careful on this narrow road with no paths. As the road turns left go straight on under the railway and turn left along the field edge with the railway to the left. Keep going bearing right, with the edge of the field past the marker post

103

to a signpost on the left.

7 Turn left, through a kissing gate along the path between hedges to the road. Take the road right to the signpost and turn left along Church Path. Bear right at the church and follow the path to Church Lane, keep ahead to Mentmore Road and turn left down to The Green and the starting point.

Background Information

The mansion at nearby Mentmore was the first of many stately homes owned in Buckinghamshire by the Rothschild family. Baron Mayer de Rothschild (1818-1874) had the house built between 1852 and 1854 to the design of Joseph Paxton the architect/engineer who had designed and built the Crystal Palace in 1851. Other members of the family built in Ascott, Aston Clinton, Waddesden, Halton and Tring Park (see walk no 4).

Hannah Rothschild (1851-1890) was his only child, she married Archibald Primrose (1847-1929) the 5th Earl of Rosebery in 1878. He was a Liberal politician who was already a rich man. Hannah died at only 39 from Bright's Disease, leaving Rosebery devastated. He had reputedly prophesied when he was a young man that he had three aims in life. The first was to marry an heiress, the second to win the Derby and the third to become Prime Minister. Hannah only saw one of these achievements; in March 1894 he succeeded Gladstone as Prime Minister and later the same year his horse, Ladas, won the Derby. He was Prime Minister for just over a year until 21st June 1895; his term of office was not a great success, but he won the Derby again that year and again in 1905.

He gave Mentmore (he hated the 'Towers' suffix and said it sounded like 'a second rate boarding house') to his son Harry (1882-1974) in the late 1920s. Harry succeeded as 6th Earl of Rosebery in 1929.

On Harry's death in 1974, Mentmore Towers and its contents were offered to the nation in lieu of £2 million inheritance tax. This was tragically turned down by James Callaghan's Government; the public were unaware then and probably still are unaware of the treasure house that was on offer. The contents were sold at an auction in 1975 for a total of £6 million.

From 1977-1997 the house belonged to the Transcendental Meditation Movement and its political offshoot the Natural Law Party.

The mansion has been a background star in several films ('Batman Begins', 'Brazil' and 'Eyes Wide Shut') and a Spice Girls music video.

30 Cow Roast

Aldbury – Tring Station – Wigginton – Cow Roast – Grand Union Canal – Tom's Hill

7 Miles	**3¼ Hours**

Location and Parking Aldbury is between the A41 near Tring and west of the B4506 at the edge of the Ashridge Estate. There is sometimes room in the car park on Stocks Lane.

Grid Reference SP965124.

Ordnance Survey Explorer Map no 181, Landranger Map no 165.

Facilities No toilets. Shop/Post Office, pubs the 'Greyhound' and the 'Valiant Trooper'.

Start The centre of the village close to the pond.

Description A more complicated walk, varied scenery and infrastructure, some stiff slopes up and down, several stiles and gates. Good paths, easy to follow and well marked.

The Walk

1 Walk out of the village along Station Road, go past the church to the signpost and turn right, through the kissing gate. Cross the open ground and go through the gate. Continue up the gravel path, through the next kissing gate and follow the path between the farm buildings and the trees. Carry on upslope along the enclosed path and through the kissing gate at the junction of paths.

2 Turn left downslope on the narrow path between hedges and keep straight on at the crossroads of paths, through the narrow gate. Continue straight on down the roadside path across the railway at Tring Station.

3 At the junction, just past the canal bridge, turn left into Beggars Lane for 400yds to the Ridgeway signpost and turn right through the kissing gate. Go along the path between the fence and the hedge to the A4251 (the old A41). Cross the road carefully, it is busier than it seems and turn right along the roadside path to the signpost.

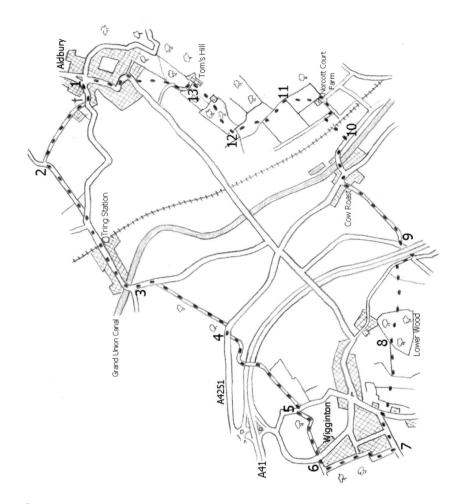

4 Take the path uphill signposted The Twist, past the barrier and through the kissing gate. Bear right up the path, turn right then left across the graceful footbridge over the dual carriageway A41. Carry on along the path, through the kissing gate and up the left hand field edge to the marker post. Turn left through this kissing gate and right, up the path between the fences and the hedge. Pass through the kissing gate at the top on to the road (The Twist) and turn right for 20yds to the signpost.

5 Go up the steps, through the kissing gate and along the footpath up the slope through the next kissing gate. Continue ahead on the field edge with the trees to the right through the top corner (kissing gate), past yet another kissing gate. Keep direction with the field edge now left past the Ordnance Survey marker point to the road at the edge of Wigginton.

6   Cross and continue ahead on the gravel path, turn left at the wooden gate down the hardcore path between the hedge and the wood. Cross the tarmac driveway and follow the path right then left between the fence and the hedge with an open field to the right.

7   At the signpost, turn left down the road with the houses to the left and carry on to the end. Turn right, to the signpost on the left, pass through the kissing gate and follow the path through the long grass downhill. Keep direction down the left hand field edge past the signpost to Cow Roast.

8   Follow the track through Lower Wood and keep direction with the electric fence to the bottom of the slope. Go through the kissing gate and bear slight left over the field which may be under cultivation although a path should be well marked. On the far side of this kissing gate turn right parallel to the A41, go down the concrete track to the road and turn left through the underpass to the signpost on the right.

9   Go through the gate and follow the hardcore road past the dogleg at the marker post, continue down to the road. Turn right, past the 'Cow Roast' inn and immediate left past the phone box, cross the bridge over the canal and turn right with the road to the signpost on the left.

10 Step over the stile in the small gap and cross the field ahead (a track should be visible). Cross the footbridge over the railway and the field ahead, turn right between the fence and the hedge to the corner. Turn left along this track and bear right at Norcott Court Farm, take the driveway left past the footpath signboard and turn right between the barn and the fence. Go over the stile and take a left hand diagonal up to the top left corner.

11 Go over the stile and carry on with the high wire fence to the right; the path goes on a slight downslope through the gap in the corner and bear right up to the stile. Take the path bearing left upslope through the field, over the stile at the top left and carry on for 50yds to the four way signpost.

12 Turn right through the metal gate, carry on ahead through the trees and keep direction on the more substantial road through Tom's Hill to the signpost on the left.

13 Turn left, the path curves left then back to the right, keeping the fence to the left. At the next signpost, go straight on over the stile and take a left hand diagonal to the opposite corner on to the road. Turn right and follow the road left to the 'Valiant Trooper, then right, back to the centre of Aldbury village.

Background Information

Cow Roast is derived from 'cow rest'; before the advent of the canal and the railway, large herds of cattle from Wales and the border area would be driven by road down to London, using the Tring Gap to cross the Chilterns. The herds and their drovers rested at the hostelry here on the summit before continuing their journey.

The railway here is the West Coast Main Line between London (Euston) and Birmingham, the North West and Scotland. It was one of the first main lines to be built and the first main line into London.

The London and Birmingham Railway was authorised in 1833 and construction started in November that year.   The chief engineer was Robert Stephenson (1803-1859), the son of railway pioneer George Stephenson, who had surveyed optional routes and decided to take the present course rather than a route via Oxford preferred by some backers.

Work proceeded smoothly in most locations but trouble was encountered at Kilsby in Northamptonshire close to Blisworth, where the Grand Union Canal had run into problems over thirty years earlier. To ease the gradients through the Chilterns at the Tring Gap, the railway navvies dug the massive cutting over 40ft deep and two and a half miles long, purely with shovels and pickaxes and took the soil away in wheelbarrows.

The 112 mile long railway was opened in 1838, 20,000 men had been working for the five years of construction, at a cost of £5½ million. It connected in Birmingham with the Grand Junction Railway on which passengers could travel further to Liverpool or Manchester. The two railways merged in 1846 to form the London and North Western Railway.

In the early part of the 20th century the LNWR was the largest joint stock company in the world and promoted itself as 'The Premier Line'.

Early railways were built on a trunk and branch system, the main line took the shortest, fastest and most easily built route between main towns.   Branches were then added to feed the trunk line from less important towns. Tring Station is consequently still in the countryside two miles away from the town centre, (a small settlement has built up around it). The station at Leighton Buzzard is across the river and the canal, a mile from the town centre. An exception is Northampton where the railway planned to go through the town but gave up after opposition from local people.

31 Woburn Abbey

Woburn Park – Eversholt – Woburn Abbey

6 Miles	**3 Hours**

Parking and Location   Woburn village is south west of Milton Keynes at the junction of the A4012 with the A5130. Use the car park on Park Street.
Grid Reference   SP950332.
Ordnance Survey   Explorer Map no 192, Landranger Map no 165.
Facilities   No toilets; pubs, shops, restaurants and takeaways in the town.
Start   From the car park.
Description   An easy, fairly level walk through the park and past the Abbey; some slight slopes and several stiles and gates. The route between points **6** and **7** is along a surprisingly busy road.

The Walk

1   Leave the car park by the vehicle entrance and turn right, go through the narrow gate next to the stone lions and bear right into the trees. Continue right/ahead along the tarmac road past the houses, over the cattle grid, straight on left of the farm buildings and through the wooden barriers.

2   Bear left at the marker post, past the end of the lake and the signboard. Carry on ahead along the track through the grass, over the access driveway, veering left closer to the road. Keep ahead through the gates at the cattle grid and bear right along Froxfield. Continue for just over a quarter of a mile to the signpost on the left just past the end of the cottages at Hills End.

3   Turn left down the wide hedged path, through the gate and continue ahead across the field which may be under cultivation although a path should be well marked. At the yellow top marker post go through the wide hedge and the dip, turn right over the footbridge and keep direction on the left hand field edge with the hedge to the left. Go through the gate slight right of the cottages and continue up the gravel drive to the

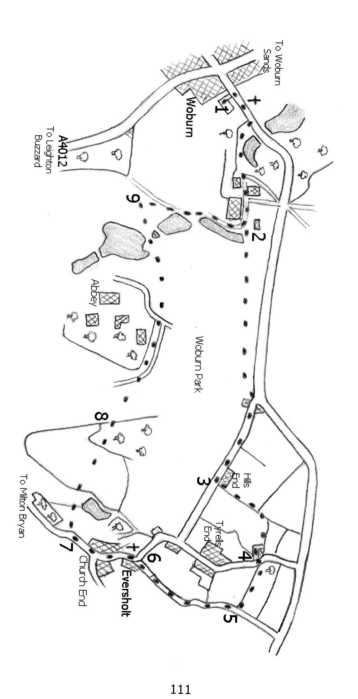

To Woburn Sands

Woburn

To Leighton Buzzard

A4012

Abbey

Woburn Park

Hills End

Tyrells End

To Milton Bryan

Church End

Eversholt

road.

4   Turn left for 75yds to the signpost and take the track on the left hand field edge through the gate and carry on along the narrow hedged path. Keep ahead on the right hand field edge through the wide gap and on to the wide grass bridleway.

5   Turn right and walk along this track around the double bend to where it can get very wet, an alternative is to take the path on the parallel field edge to the right. Keep ahead on the tarmac track into Church End, Eversholt.

6   Take the road left/straight on through the village past the church and keep right on the main road at the junction. Continue for 340yds to the footpath signpost and turn right, through the high kissing gate.

7   Bear right to the notice board and follow the path on a left hand diagonal, through the gate at the midway point to the trees on the far side. Bear right through the boundary and cross the narrow field, go up the steps in the hedge and continue straight on along the path upslope between fields. Follow the path through the trees and exit via the high kissing gate on the far side.

8   Keep direction and carry on parallel to the tarmac estate road, between the abbey and the car park. Go past the no entry signs, along the chain fenced tarmac drive and past marker posts. Maintain direction between the lakes for another 300yds to a marker post marked only with an arrow straight on.

9   Turn right across to the yellow topped post left of the lake and bear right past the end of the lake. Go through the Woburn Abbey ticket barriers to the corner and turn left. Retrace your steps past the farm buildings and through the trees to the starting point in the car park.

Background Information

Woburn Abbey was founded in 1145 as part of the Cistercian Order. The Abbey flourished during the Middle Ages but was suppressed by King Henry VIII at the Reformation.

The Russell family came to Woburn in 1547 when it was given to Sir John Russell by King Henry VIII. Sir John had held several important political offices under the King and was one of the executors of his will. He became one of the counsellors of the new King, ten year old Edward VI. In 1551 he was created Earl of Bedford for his services to the young King and his backing for the new Protestant religion.

Francis Russell (1593-1641) the 4th Earl, succeeded his cousin in 1627. He was active politically in the run up to the Civil War. The Earl was also the leader of a group of 'adventurers', rich men who put up capital to drain the Cambridgeshire Fens for new farming land. The new land between Earith and Downham Market is called the Bedford level, drained by the New Bedford and the Old Bedford Rivers.

Francis's son William (1616-1700) followed his father in siding with Parliament in the Civil War. He fought with the Parliamentarians at Edge Hill in 1642, but changed his allegiance in 1643 and was on the Royalist side at battles in Gloucester and Newbury. He was back however with Parliament in December. The roundheads never really trusted him again and he took no further part in the war.

The second half of the century brought mixed blessings to the Earl. In 1683 his son William, the MP for Bedfordshire was implicated in the Rye House Plot and beheaded at the Tower. After the accession of William and Mary as sovereigns in the Glorious Revolution of 1688, William was given a posthumous pardon. The Earl was created Duke of Bedford in 1694.

The present house was built under the direction of the 4th Duke between 1747 and 1761 by the architect Henry Flitcroft. Further building by Henry Holland took place in 1786-88. The gardens and parkland were laid out by Humphry Repton in 1802.

Francis, the 5th Duke (1765-1802) died suddenly without marrying; he had been expected to marry Lady Georgiana Gordon, but the engagement had not been announced. He was succeeded by his younger brother John (1766-1839) who was already a widower with three small children. He later married Lady Georgiana who was of course upset that her son would not succeed as Duke. The Duke's youngest son by his first marriage, Lord John Russell, was Prime Minister from 1846-52 and 1865-66.

Ian Russell (1917-2002), 13th Duke from 1953, inherited a Woburn partly derelict and a liability for death duties for the second time in thirteen years. He set about making the stately home pay its way and created one of the country's major tourist attractions, following the successful throwing open of the doors of the house to the paying public, with a magnificent Safari Park containing an eclectic mix of wild animals.

Nature Notes

The high gates and cattle grids leading into Woburn Park confine several herds of non indigenous deer. The rarest of these, Pere David's Deer (discovered by the French missionary in 1865) became extinct in the wild in their native China. Woburn sent a small herd to China in 1985 to be re-introduced in a forest close to Beijing.

32 Church Lock

Slapton – River Ouzel – Church Lock – Grand Union Canal

4¼ Miles   2 Hours

Location and Parking Slapton is between the A4146 at Billington and the B488 at Horton. No car park, use a sensibly located roadside space.

Grid Reference SP934208.

Ordnance Survey Explorer Map no 192, Landranger Map no 165.

Facilities None.

Start In the centre of the village, at the T-junction of Horton Road, Church Road and Mill Road.

Description A flat easy walk out along the banks of the River Ouzel, returning on the towpath of the Grand Union Canal. Some gates and stiles, the route between points **2** and **3** can sometimes get overgrown making the going a little bit harder.

The Walk

1   Leave along Mill Road, go through the kissing gate between the road and the last house; keep direction, with the hedge and the road to the right, over the farm driveway and the stile in the hedge gap, into the far corner. Turn left down to the signpost, turn right through the boundary and take the road to the right over the bridge.

2   Cross the stile on the left, follow the bank of the River Ouzel and continue between the river and the embankment to a marker post in front of a hedge across the track. Turn sharp right, go over the three sleeper bridge and turn left again between the river and the embankment. Step over the stile/footbridge and keep ahead through this ridged, undulating field.

3   Go over the stile; turn left along the field edge over the next stile and cross the field slight left. Step over the stile up onto the canal towpath and turn left, walk up to Bridge 116 and cross the canal.

4   Turn left along the towpath past Church Lock with the canal now to

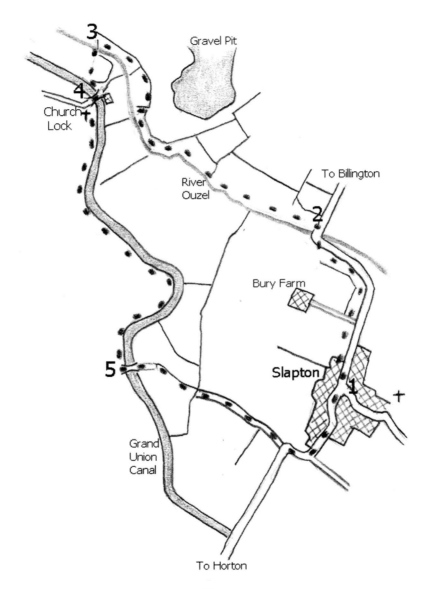

the left. Follow the towpath for a mile and a quarter to the next bridge and cross the canal.

5 Walk up the left hand field edge and cross the stile next to the metal gate; keep ahead along the wide hedged farm track to the road at a bend. Follow the road to the junction and turn left back into the village and the starting point.

Background Information

In the early days of transportation by canal the people who ran the narrow boats were quite prosperous. An owner or operator would employ a crew or helper; at least two people were needed, one to lead and look after the horse and one to steer the boat. Wives and families stayed on shore in their own house. When the railways arrived with shorter, quicker and often cheaper freight services, canal tolls came down and canal workers found life a lot more difficult. The easiest way to reduce costs was to close down any household on land and take the family on canal journeys to act as crew. The most usual combination would be the husband looking after the horse on the towpath and the wife steering the boat, often holding the tiller under her arm or using her feet, so that she could get on with a piece of crochet work or tie up old pieces of towline into fenders or ropework. Older children would often help out or be loaned to another family to help them.

Living accommodation was cramped, the canals were nominally seven feet wide, so the cabin would be six feet wide by nine or ten feet long, making them smaller then the average modern touring caravan. Life must have been hard with small children to keep out of the water and a cabin which boat wives prided themselves in keeping spotlessly clean in difficult conditions. The boats would often have a dirty cargo like coal, to be delivered to a filthy wharf in a grimy industrial area.

It was even worse when the boats themselves began to be powered by steam engines continually belching out smutty, dusty smoke. The advantage of steam or diesel power was of course that the main boat would be able to tow a second boat and double the carrying capacity; the second unpowered boat is called a butty. Narrow boats are always boats never barges; barges are larger, wider and work mainly on rivers pulled by tugboats.

It became an insular, almost closed world where canal people were regarded with suspicion by outsiders; they stuck together and supported one another. The children were normally illiterate because of the difficulties of regular schooling and intermarried within the canal community. The way that canal workers dressed was usually very distinctive; the women wearing long skirts, shawls and elaborate white bonnets long after they became unfashionable.

The origin of the traditional decoration of canal boats with designs incorporating roses and stylised castles has been already lost. It is possible that the roses symbolise the gardens missing from their narrowboats and the castles signify large and roomy places to live. The decoration was always completed on a fairly amateur basis, carried out by boatbuilders rather than professional artists or signwriters and often by the boatmen themselves.

Modern boats are built slightly narrower than older boats as some locks have subsided and made easy passage a little more difficult. The older working boats were also sometimes 72ft long; builders are now keeping designs at 60ft so that boats can go almost anywhere on the British canal system. Newly built or converted boats are incredibly luxurious compared to working boats, but they do have a lot more room using all of the original cargo area as well as the cabin. Some are so well appointed that it is possible to take a bath inside as well as outside the hull.

33 Ivinghoe Beacon

The Ridgeway National Trail – Ivinghoe Beacon – Icknield Way

4¼ Miles   **2 Hours**

Location and Parking Use the car park 500yds southeast of the path to the top of Ivinghoe Beacon on the minor road past the Beacon between the B489 and the B4506.
Grid Reference SP963159
Ordnance Survey Explorer Map no 181, Landranger Map no 165.
Facilities None.
Start From the car park.
Description Good paths, well marked; some gates and stiles; two sharp slopes and a steep set of steps.

The Walk

1 Leave the car park entrance to the left (southeast towards the B4506) along the path through the trees on the left hand side of the road for 380yds to the signpost set back from the road on the right. Take the path downhill through the trees across the stile and on to the Ridgeway Path.

2 Turn right upslope again passing left of the stile, past a marker post along the path through the low trees down to the signpost. Bear right, through the kissing gate uphill, then down to the road.

3 Cross and follow the path to the top of Ivinghoe Beacon, bear right along the top of the ridge, through the kissing gate and down to the stile ahead. Turn right, down the side of the ridge; step over the stile next to the double gates to the junction by the trees.

4 Turn right along the path between fields past the trees to the kissing gate at the end. (The path slight right up the hill leads directly back to the starting point in the car park above). Bear left to the marker post and turn left through the kissing gate and into the trees.

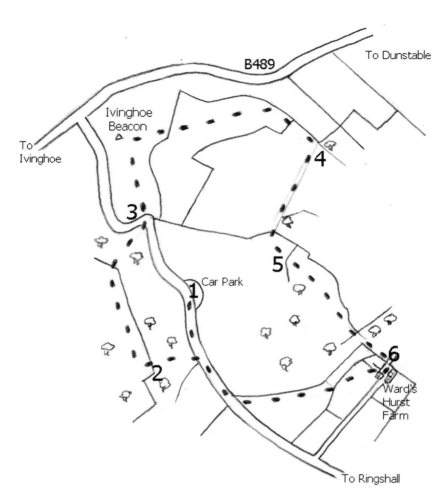

5 Carry on along the path through the trees, past the bigger than normal marker post and up the flight of steps. At the top continue ahead with the fence to the right up to the farm road.

6 Turn right, past the wooden posts and right again past the vehicles to the gate on the left. Pass through and turn right on the right hand field edge with the trees to the right, through the boundary to the gate at the far right corner. Turn right along the path through the trees on the right of the road, back to the starting point in the car park.

Background Information

Ivinghoe Beacon at 817ft is one of the highest points of the Chilterns and a popular viewpoint for visitors to the area. Also the site of a Tudor warning beacon and a prehistoric hillfort, it is well known as the junction of the Ridgeway Path and the Icknield Way.

The Ridgeway Path became a National Trail in 1973; running for 87 miles from Overton Hill, near Avebury to Ivinghoe Beacon. It is part of the long distance footpath from Lyme Regis on the Dorset Coast to Holme on the Norfolk coast near Hunstanton. The Wessex Ridgeway links Overton Hill with Lyme Regis; it continues from Ivinghoe Beacon as the Icknield Way to Knettishall on the Norfolk/Suffolk border. It joins Peddars Way, which like most roads of Roman origin runs in a straight line to North Norfolk. The word Icknield is derived from the Saxon word for upper road.

The route is at least 5,000 years old, along high ground and away from the low, marshy valleys which became impassable in winter. Fewer trees grew on the land along the ridges, so travellers were at less risk from thieves, outlaws and brigands hiding in woodland. The thoroughfare must have been busy with trade and transport during prehistoric times connecting local hillforts with other ancient settlements.

The trackway fell out of use during the Roman occupation, the invaders preferring to build their own road system to suit their civilisation. It started to be used again after the Romans had gone, Saxon and Viking invaders finding it useful for getting their raiding parties quickly from place to place. Later it was used by cattle drovers moving their herds from Wales and the West Country to market in London. The track would have been very open until the Enclosures of agricultural land took place in the 18th century. Hedges and earth banks were put into position to stop animals in these herds from damaging crops and land.

34 Gade Valley

Jockey End – Hoo Wood – Great Gaddesden – Gaddesden Place – Golden Parsonage

6 Miles   3 Hours

Location and Parking Jockey End is on a minor road, parallel with and midway between the A4146 and the A5 at Markyate. No car park, find a sensibly located roadside space, there is often room near the phone box.
Grid Reference TL040137
Ordnance Survey Explorer Map no 182, Landranger Map no 166.
Facilities None.
Start The junction near the phone box. Two noticeable slopes, several stiles and gates. Check in wet weather that the Gade Valley is not flooded; if it is impassable detour via the A4146.

The Walk

1 Take the road towards Studham for 60yds to the signpost, turn left over the footbridge/stile and walk up the field edge with the hedge to the right. Step over the stile in the corner and bear left through the wide gap and right, to the road.

2 Turn right, to the signpost and go down the driveway left through the trees. Bear left of the house at the marker discs and follow the path bearing right, through a fence gap. Cross the field, which may be under cultivation, on a path leading away from the hedge diagonally left, a path should be well marked within any crop. Go through the hedge gap and turn left through the boundary.

3 Follow the fenced path along the field edge to the next boundary. Step over the stile and take a right hand diagonal about halfway along the far fence. Walk along the field edge with the fence to the left and continue in the next field with Hoo Wood to the right, carry on ahead through the kissing gate and the trees.

4 Bear left out through the kissing gate and cross the field (a path

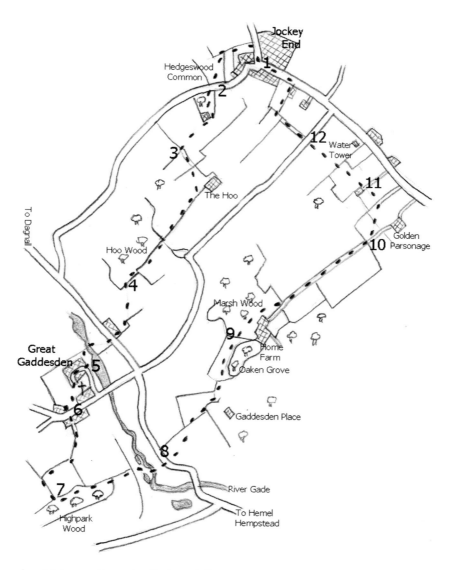

should be well marked) downhill on a right hand diagonal left of the corner. Follow the path along the field edge bearing right, down to the A4146. Cross this busy road carefully and step over the stile opposite, bear right over the footbridges over the River Gade and take a left hand diagonal to the stile by the signpost at the top left.

5 Turn right uphill on the road, bearing left to the signpost, cross the stile, turn left through the kissing gate and bear right across the new cemetery. Continue through both kissing gates at the top left, carry on uphill over a stile and turn left; descend the steps to the road and turn right.

6 At the signpost take the wide track left; go through the kissing gate and up the left hand field edge through the next kissing gate. Bear right on the right hand field edge with the hedge to the right and turn right at the corner, hedge still right up to the boundary. Turn left along the left hand field edge to High Park Wood.

7 Go through the gap into the wood, bear left and turn left, through the trees downhill. Continue between hedges, through a kissing gate and bear right across the footbridge back across the Gade. Exit through the kissing gate to the road and cross with care.

8 Pass through the gate, step over the stile and bear left uphill; follow the track in the grass to the stile and cross this and the stile immediately left. Carry on uphill through the gate at the top and keep ahead through the next gate. Turn left, across the stile in the dip and maintain direction parallel with the telegraph poles, bearing right and go through the wide wooden gate.

9 Follow the wide track through the trees and out the other side, continue left/straight on along the stony farm road for half a mile to the half green gate.

10 Bear left across the field, go through the kissing gate and keep direction through the next kissing gate on the left. Turn right on the enclosed path, go through the gap and turn left along the field edge with the hedge to the left.

11 Take the tarmac drive to the left and an immediate right at the signpost. Keep ahead slight left over a series of stiles and step over the stiles at the line of trees. (The water tower is off to the right). Continue between fields through a kissing gate to the road.

12 Turn right and immediate left, through the narrow metal gate, follow the path, between fences through the dip and keep ahead over a stile into an open field. Go along the right hand field edge for 40yds and turn right over the stile, walk along the wide path past the overgrown allotments all the way to the road. Turn left along the roadside path back to Jockey End and the starting point.

Background Information

The Halsey family have owned the Gaddesden Estate since the 16th century. They originally lived in the house now known as 'The Golden Parsonage'; the Palladian Mansion 'Gaddesden Place' designed and built by Thomas Wyatt was completed in 1774. The gardens and parkland at Gaddesden Place and The Hoo were both landscaped by Capability Brown.

35 Blow's Down

Dunstable – Blow's Down – Caddington

6½ Miles	3¼ Hours

Location and Parking   Use any car park in Dunstable although Church Street would be the most convenient, (pay and display).
Grid Reference   TL019219
Ordnance Survey   Explorer Map no 193, Landranger Map no 166.
Facilities   All facilities available close by in the town.
Start   The crossroads in the town centre where the A505 joins the A5.
Description   A stiff slope up onto the Downs close to the start, otherwise fairly level.   Some stiles and gates, the route is easy to follow on downland, field edges and well surfaced bridleways.

The Walk

1   Walk east along Church Street past Priory Road; just before the railway bridge turn right into Station Road. Go up to the corner and turn slight left to the Icknield Way signpost, take the path ahead through the undergrowth at the backs of the houses. Bear right of the first pylon, go under the second pylon and continue to the green metal gate where the road from the right ends.
2   Continue ahead through the wooden kissing gate at the signpost pointing to Caddington and bear right along the path right of the pylons. Level with the first pylon, fork left up the (unmarked), less well used path rising diagonally upslope, passing a marker post and left of the next pylon. At the top of the slope carry on with the fence to the left, through the kissing gate and the bushes.
3   Turn left through the hedge gap at the marker post and continue the original direction with the hedge now right. Bear left with the field edge past the end of Dame Ellen's Wood and turn right along the tarmac farm road to the marker post.
4   Take the field edge to the left, with the hedge on the right bearing right, down to the corner. Bear left through the gap and turn right,

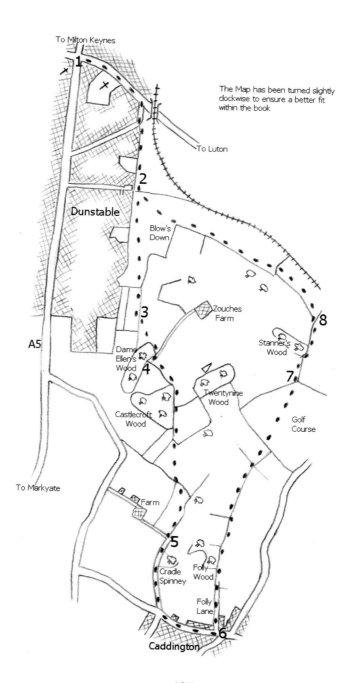

To Milton Keynes

1

To Luton

The Map has been turned slightly
clockwise to ensure a better fit
within the book

2

Dunstable

Blow's
Down

3

Zouches
Farm

8

A5

Dame
Ellen's
Wood

Stanner's
Wood

4

7

Twentynine
Wood

Castlecroft
Wood

Golf
Course

To Markyate

Farm

5

Cradle
Spinney

Folly
Wood

Folly
Lane

6

Caddington

down the field edge parallel to the telegraph poles. Go through the wide gap at the marker post and carry on ahead over the field still close to the telegraph poles. Continue through the boundary and bear left on the track across the grass, at the field edge bear right down to the corner, go through the gate and down the steps to the hedged bridleway.

5 Turn left and immediate right along the wide sunken track with overhanging trees and carry on to the road at the edge of Caddington village. Take the roadside path left to Folly Lane and turn left.

6 Continue straight on when the tarmac road stops, along the field edge with Folly Wood to the left. At the narrow hedge gap turn left, then right to continue direction with the hedge now to the right. In the corner go through the wooden barrier and keep ahead across the golf course, cross a stony road and bear left (carefully) over a fairway. Carry on past a marker post up to the wooden barrier in the top corner and out of the golf course.

7 Maintain direction along the right hand field edge, past the end of Stanner's Wood; carry on with the hedge still left and bear left at the marker post down the narrow tunnelled path through the kissing gate to the marker post.

8 Turn left on the path along the top of Blow's Down, bear left of the marker post with the hedge and the fence to the left; step over the stile and continue ahead on the higher path past marker posts and through a kissing gate. At an unmarked point, fork right downhill to the bottom corner close to the information board at point 2 and retrace the route back into Dunstable and the starting point.

Background Information

Dunstable Priory was the location of an event to have far reaching effects on English history. At a court held there on 23rd May 1533 Thomas Cranmer annulled the marriage of King Henry VIII and Katherine of Aragon. Cranmer had been Archbishop of Canterbury for only a few weeks, he had been a surprise choice for the job having held no important positions in the church. He owed much to his friendship with the Boleyn family and Henry's belief that he would support his petition.

The Priory was also the site of an overnight stop in the funeral cortege of Eleanor of Castile (1241-1290), the wife of King Edward I. The couple married in 1254 and enjoyed an unusually happy relationship in what had been a dynastically arranged marriage. Eleanor always travelled with Edward during his various journeys; she was with him on a crusade from 1270-1274 and gave birth to the future Edward II at Caernarfon while on campaign in Wales.

She died in Harby, Nottinghamshire, in November 1290. Her body was carried in solemn procession to Westminster Abbey for internment. The funeral cortege stopped overnight on twelve occasions; Edward later had a cross erected at each of these locations in commemoration of his late wife. Nothing survives of the Cross at Dunstable although a new modernistic statue of the queen has been placed in the Queen Eleanor Shopping Centre.

There were three other crosses in the immediate area at St Albans, Woburn and Stony Stratford. Only three crosses survive, at Waltham Cross, Northampton and the best preserved at Geddington in Northamptonshire.

The Charing Cross was where the equestrian statue of Charles II stands south of Trafalgar Square; the original cross was destroyed by the Puritans who considered it to be an example of idolatry. The present cross was erected by the London Chatham and Dover Railway in front of their new hotel at Charing Cross Station.

Nature Notes

The Ring Ouzel, a member of the Thrush family but far less common than its cousins can often be seen on Blow's Down. Much like a Blackbird but slightly smaller and slimmer; the wings have pale edges and seem lighter when folded, but the main identification is a broad white crescent on the chest. The female has browner plumage and the crescent is not as distinct. They are much less tame or friendly than a Blackbird and may be seen from a distance standing on a rock, singing, but will quickly fly away.

36 Incombe Hole

Ivinghoe – Ivinghoe Beacon – Incombe Hole

4¼ Miles   2½ Hours

Location and Parking   Ivinghoe is on the B489 between Dunstable and Aston Clinton at the junction with the B488. No car park, find a sensibly located roadside space.
Grid Reference   SP945161
Ordnance Survey   Explorer Map no 181, Landranger Map no 165.
Facilities   No toilets. Pubs the 'Rose and Crown' and the 'Bell'; post office in Ivinghoe, bigger shop in Pitstone.
Start   From the junction by the church.
Description   Not an easy walk. Good paths, well marked and easy to follow. Several stiles and gates. The path up the side of the Beacon is steep and tough; the view from the top makes it worthwhile; there are other slopes up and down.

The Walk

1   Go along Church Road (towards Dunstable) and turn left into Vicarage Road. At the 'Rose and Crown' turn right into Wellcroft and continue straight on up the stony bridleway between hedges. Continue direction for a mile and a quarter, past Crabtree Cottage, to the road.
2   Turn right and go through the kissing gate, follow the left hand field edge upslope with the hedge to the left. At the marker post, turn right and go through the kissing gate. Carry on with the fence to the right to the top right corner. Turn left uphill, fence still right over a stile and through the kissing gate to the road, turn right along the roadside path.
3   Take the road left, signposted to Ashridge; go over the cattle grid to the signpost and turn left. Climb one of the steep paths up the side of Ivinghoe Beacon, at the top turn right along the gentler slope to the road.
4   Cross and continue straight on to the marker post, take the wider

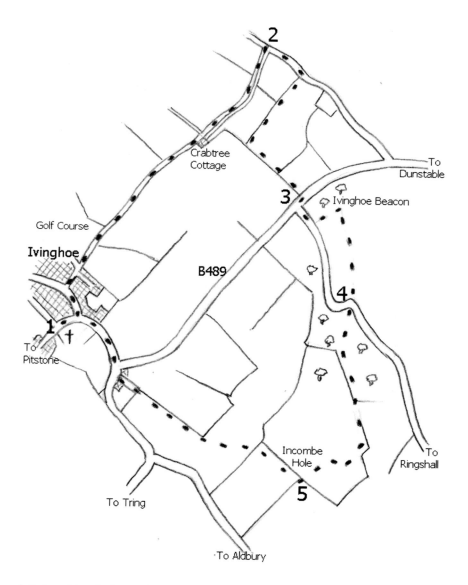

left hand track through the trees and bushes. Keep ahead over the stile next to the gate, down slope to the marker post. Bear right after 90yds, then left on the path around the edge of Incombe Hole.

5 Bear right with the path still on the edge but moving further away, keeping ahead across the stile. Bear left past the end of the hedge and follow the track right, through the grass and keep ahead with the hedge to the right. At the bottom continue down the fenced path to the road. Follow the roadside path to the right, back into Ivinghoe and your starting point.

Background Information

The windmill at Pitstone is owned by the National Trust and open on Sunday afternoons through the summer. The mill is believed to be the oldest in this country as it has the date 1627 carved inside. It may however be older as wooden mills are subject to constant renovation and repair. It is a post mill, the upper, wooden part of the mill containing the milling machinery is pivoted on a substantial post and the whole thing turned to catch the wind.

In 1902 the mill was badly damaged by a gale and considered to be not worth the cost of repair. A local farmer bought the ruins of the mill from the Ashridge Estate when it was being sold off in the early 1920s; he gave it to the National Trust in 1937.

The mill remained derelict until 1963 when a group of National Trust members started to restore the mill to working condition. The mill reopened in 1970.

37 Sharpenhoe Clappers

Mill End – Pulloxhill – Sharpenhoe Clappers

8¼ Miles **4 Hours**

Location and Parking Sharpenhoe village is off the A6 west of Barton-le-Clay, use the car park at Sharpenhoe Clappers at the top of the slope south of the village on the road to Streatley.
Grid Reference TL065295
Ordnance Survey Explorer Map no 193, Landranger Map no 166.
Facilities None. Pub the 'Lynmore' in the village.
Start From the car park.
Description Good paths, mostly well marked; stiles and several gates. There is a sharp slope downhill near the start and a long easy slope up to Pulloxhill. The walk finishes with a tough slope up to the Clappers.

The Walk
1 Walk out of the car park, cross the road and ascend the steps. Go through the kissing gate and bear slight left, over the stile in the opposite fence. Follow the path left with the ground sloping away to the right, around to the marker post pointing downhill.
The water tower ahead is at point 7 of the walk.
2 Take the path downslope through the kissing gate at the bottom, keep ahead on the right hand field edge and follow the track left in the corner, with the hedge still to the right, up to the footbridge. Cross and keep ahead on the wide farm track, follow this track bearing right through the wide gap in the corner.
3 Bear left along the left hand field edge with the trees now to the left. Turn right in the corner and continue along this left hand field edge all the way to the road at Mill End. Follow the road left for 300yds, over the bridge and up to the byway signpost.
4 Go along the wide grass track to the right past the metal barrier and marker post, bearing right, uphill. Turn left and follow this hedged track to Upper Samshill Farm and turn left along the narrow tarmac road.

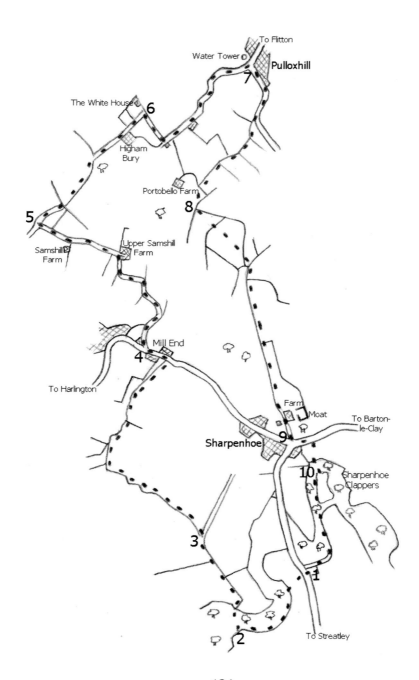

To Flitton

Water Tower **Pulloxhill**

7

The White House 6

Higham
Bury

Portobello Farm

8

5

Upper Samshill
Farm

Samshill
Farm

Mill End

4

To Harlington

Farm

Moat

9 To Barton-
le-Clay

Sharpenhoe

10

Sharpenhoe
Clappers

3

1

2

To Streatley

5 As this road swings left, turn right at the signpost along the hardcore track, after 80yds turn right at the marker post up the narrower hedged track. Continue ahead up the right hand field edge with the hedge to the right. At the yellow top post, turn right, through the metal gate; go up the left hand field edge and through the gate on the left. Keep direction with the hedge to the right, past the wall and up to the road at the White House.

6 Turn right on the tarmac road to the T-junction and take the road left to the junction at the water tower in Pulloxhill.

7 Take Blackhill Road to the right, along the tarmac road and past the metal barrier, bearing right, to the corner. Sharpenhoe Clappers can usually be seen ahead. As this wide track swings left bear right along the right hand field edge with the hedge to the right. At the corner bear right past the marker post, over the two sleeper bridge and keep ahead past a marker post up the hedged path. Carry on along the right hand field edge and go through two metal kissing gates. Bear left through another kissing gate and take a right hand diagonal to the bottom corner.

8 Turn left through the kissing gate and continue through the kissing gate in the fence opposite, go straight on to the kissing gate ahead, go through and turn right with the hedge to the right. Cross the footbridge and keep direction along the wide farm track, past the white house and up the drive to the road.

9 Cross and turn left along the roadside path for 200yds to the signpost. Turn right, up the field edge through the gap in the corner and ascend the steep steps in the trees up to Sharpenhoe Clappers.

10 Bear right and follow the path around the rim; continue out of the trees and turn right between the fence and the trees back to the car park and the starting point.

Background Information

The 525ft high, wooded spur of Sharpenhoe Clappers is one of the most distinctive features of the northern Chilterns; it can easily be seen why this site was chosen as a defensive point during the Iron Age. The Clappers must have been well known to the 17th century author John Bunyan; the hill is reputed to be the 'Delectable Mountains' of his classic work 'The Pilgrim's Progress'.

William Robertson was the eldest of four brothers born in Kensington in the 1870s. He was a successful barrister who died unmarried in 1937. In his will he left money to the National Trust to be used to purchase land or property in memory of his two youngest brothers, Norman and Laurance, who died in the First World War. Two Bedfordshire properties benefited from this legacy, both with memorials as specified in William Robertson's will (see notes on walk no 16, Dunstable Downs). Sharpenhoe Clappers was bought by the Trust in 1939; the memorial is in the trees on top of the hill.

Index

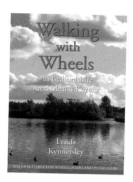

WALKING WITH WHEELS
in Bedfordshire and Milton Keynes
Lynda Kynnersley

Access. The walks have all been chosen for their ease of access with as much information as possible about the physical features of the route, to enable people with limited mobility to decide for themselves whether a particular walk is within their ability. Some walks are on trails that have been specially adapted to make them more accessible but others are on country paths, which have reasonably flat, smooth and hard surfaces.

Distance. The walks vary in length from a mile and a half up to seven miles, with the possibility of extending them to up to fourteen miles. The majority of the walks are designed to be circular with different outward and return routes, but in a few cases there are no suitable return routes and the directions will say to retrace your steps to the start point. A few walks are described as linear and on these routes, you can either do the whole walk, arranging transport at each end, or start the walk at any suitable point, go as far as you choose and retrace your route..

Details of how to get to the start point, where to park and where to find refreshments are all included, as well as general information of interest about the area and what wildlife you may see - everything in fact for a good trip out.

The
Book
Castle

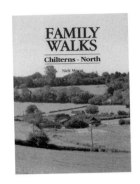

FAMILY WALKS
Chilterns – North

FAMILY WALKS
Chilterns - South
Nick Moon

A series of two books providing a comprehensive coverage of walks throughout the whole of the Chiltern area. The walks included vary in length from 1.7 to 5.5 miles, but are mainly in the 3 to 5 mile range, which is ideal for families with children, less experienced walkers or short winter afternoons.

Each walk text gives details of nearby places of interest and is accompanied by a specially drawn map of the route, which also indicates local pubs and a skeleton road network.

The author, Nick Moon, has lived in or regularly visited the Chilterns all his life and has for 25 years, been an active member of the Chiltern Society's Rights of Way Group, which seeks to protect and improve the area's footpath and bridleway network.

The
Book
Castle

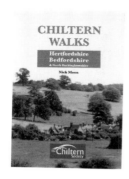
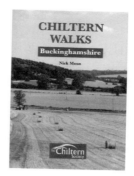
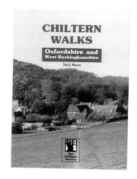

CHILTERN WALKS
Hertfordshire, Bedfordshire and North Buckinghamshire

CHILTERN WALKS
Buckinghamshire

CHILTERN WALKS
Oxfordshire and West Buckinghamshire
Nick Moon

A series of three books to providing a comprehensive coverage of walks throughout the whole of the Chiltern area (as defined by the Chiltern Society). The walks included vary in length from 3.0 to 10.9 miles, but are mainly in the 5-7 mile range popular for half-day walks, although suggestions of possible combinations of walks are given for those preferring a full day's walk.

Each walk gives details of nearby places of interest and is accompanied by a specially drawn map of the route which also indicates local pubs and a skeleton road network.

The Book Castle

143

THE CHILTERN AREA'S LEADING SERIES OF MAPS FOR WALKERS
by Nick Moon

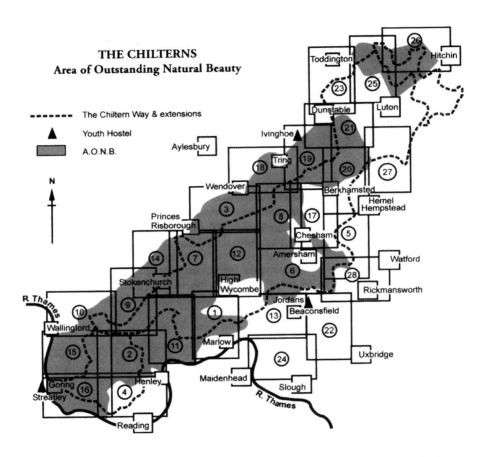

THE CHILTERNS
Area of Outstanding Natural Beauty

- - - - - - - The Chiltern Way & extensions

▲ Youth Hostel

▓ A.O.N.B.

N

This expanding series of currently 28 maps at a scale of 2½ inches to the mile depicts footpaths, bridleways and other routes available to walkers, riders and cyclists across the Chilterns, as well as pubs, railway stations, car parking facilities and other features of interest. Several suggested walks also appear on the back of each map. New titles appear regularly and will extend coverage of the area.

COMPLETE LIST OF CHILTERN SOCIETY FOOTPATH MAPS

1. High Wycombe & Marlow
2. Henley & Nettlebed
3. Wendover & Princes Risborough
4. Henley and Caversham
5. Sarratt & Chipperfield
6. Amersham & Penn Country
7. West Wycombe & Princes Risborough
8. Chartridge & Cholesbury
9. The Oxfordshire Escarpment

10. Wallingford & Watlington
11. The Hambleden Valley
12. Hughenden Valley & Gt. Missenden
13. Beaconsfield & District
14. Stokenchurch & Chinnor
15. Crowmarsh & Nuffield
16. Goring & Mapledurham
17. Chesham & Berkhamsted
18. Tring & Wendover
19. Ivinghoe & Ashridge

20. Hemel Hempstead & the Gade Valley
21. Dunstable Downs & Caddington
22. Gerrards Cross & Chalfont St. Peter
23. Toddington & Houghton Regis
24. Burnham Beeches & Stoke Poges
25. Sundon & the Barton Hills
26. Hitchin & Hexton
27. Flamstead & Redbourn
28. Rickmansworth & Chenies

EXPLORING HISTORY ALL AROUND
Vivienne Evans

A handbook of local history, arranged as a series of routes to cover Bedfordshire and adjoining parts of Hertfordshire and Buckinghamshire. It is organised as two books in one. There are seven thematic sections full of fascinating historical detail and anecdotes for armchair reading. Also it is a perfect source of family days out as the book is organised as circular motoring/cycling explorations, highlighting attractions and landmarks. Also included is a background history to all the major towns in the area, plus dozens of villages, which will enhance your appreciation and understanding of the history that is all around you!

The Book Castle

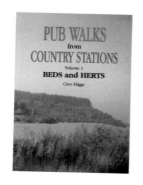
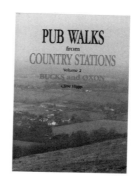

PUB WALKS FROM COUNTRY STATIONS
Volume 1 - Beds and Herts

PUB WALKS FROM COUNTRY STATIONS
Volume 2 - Bucks and Oxon
Clive Higgs

Two titles both containing fourteen circular country rambles, each starting and finishing at a railway station and incorporating a pub-stop at a mid-way point.

Volume 1 has 5 walks in Bedfordshire starting from Sandy, Biggleswade, Harlington, Flitwick and Linslade. Together with 9 walks in Hertfordshire starting from Watford, Kings Langley, Boxmoor, Berkhamsted, Tring, Stanstead St. Margaret's, Watton-at-Stone, Bricket Wood and Harpdenden.

Volume 2 has 9 walks in Buckingham starting from Gerrards Cross, Beaconsfield, Saunderton, Princes Risborough, Amersham, Chesham, Great Missenden, Stoke Manderville and Wendover. Together with 5 walks in Oxfordshire starting from Goring-on-Thames, Cholsey, Lower Shiplake, Islip and Hanborough Station.

The shortest walk is a distance of 4 miles and the longest 7 and a half miles.

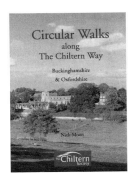
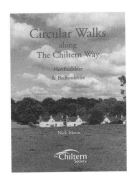

CIRCULAR WALKS ALONG
THE CHILTERN WAY

Volume One Buckinghamshire and Oxfordshire
Volume Two Hertfordshire and Bedfordshire

Nick Moon

A two volume series with special maps provided for each walk.

The walks range from 4.3 to 8.5 miles which makes for a comfortable half day or a leisurely full day walk. In addition, details of several possible combinations of walks of up to 22 miles are provided for those who would like a longer, more challenging walk.

Each walk gives details of nearby places of interest and is accompanied by a specially drawn map of the rout which also indicates local pubs and a skeleton road network.